"Jim Schaap, faithful Calvinist, teacher, writer of vivid stories, photographer of beauty wherever he finds it, focuses a yea͏ ͏his pondering on Mother Teresa's life and writings. He and sh apart in origin and influence, yet in this book he invites ͏ be called an intimately ecumenical embrace, findi͏ despite their differences. Follow his thinking a͏ book and discover what makes spiritual kin͏'

Luci Shaw, poet and e͏ ͏ly of
Adventure of Ascent: Fie͏ ͏g journey
and *Thumbprint in the Clay: Divine mar͏* ͏der and grace

"James Schaap's *Reading Mother Theresa* represents his entry into a devotional genre that breaks the mold in deliciously satisfying ways. Its confessional tone challenges the Protestant reticence to acknowledge the depth of Catholic spirituality. Its wordsmith's command of language allows for an evocative multi-layered reflection that is rarely found in works of this nature. The result is a devotional that does what good devotionals are meant to do – provoke a thoughtful piety that lingers well beyond the initial reading."

Dr. John Hubers, Professor of Religion,
Northwestern College, Orange City, IA

"Jim Schaap looks into the icon of Mother Teresa and he finds it a mirror for his own soul. The distances in culture and context between them only sharpen the images. You'll find in his reflections on her reflections a communion of sainthood that reaches out to you too. Would you do it if you heard Jesus tell you to change your clothes?"

Dr. Daniel Meeter, Pastor,
Old First Reformed Church, Brooklyn, NY

"In *Reading Mother Teresa* we discover the Catholic side of James Schaap, a Dutch Calvinist haunted by the presence of God in the sunrise and the wide expanse of the prairie sky. We also encounter the Calvinist side of Mother Teresa, a Roman Catholic deeply immersed in the darkness and depravity of a world wracked by sin. Through these meditations Schaap brings the life and faith of Mother Theresa into conversation with the world of Dutch Calvinism, affirming that it is in difference where life is most interesting. More than that, Schaap shows how human experience transcends the boundaries of history, geography, and tradition, and how the promise of Christ's resurrection comes to us in peculiarly ordinary ways. Spend some time with Schaap and Mother Theresa – an odd couple, for sure, but a journey worth taking."

Dr. Jason Lief, Assistant Professor of Theology, Dordt College,author of *Poetic Youth Ministry: Learning to love young people by letting them go*

"Jim Schaap reaches into his own walk and others, into the Protestant (read Calvinistic) and Roman Catholic traditions, into the paradoxes of the Christian faith – 'truth always has two centers' – and into writings by authors, some deemed classic, others well on the way, and put together a volume of meditations on walking with Christ through the lens of Mother Teresa's life. The life and work of Mother Teresa deserves to be studied, Schaap's meditations counsel, a woman who swore 'not to refuse [God] anything.'"

Doug Calsbeek, Editor,
Orange City Capital-Democrat, Orange City, IA

"We love reading James Schaap on the quirks of the Dutch Reformed on the prairie, or perhaps the travails of Native Americans. But a Roman Catholic saint? This book isn't so much 'about' Mother Teresa, as it is about Schaap's encounter, maybe even dance, with Teresa. Suffering is a prevalent theme, but always tempered by Schaap's expected wit, warmth, and authenticity."

Steve Mathonnet-Vander Wel, Pastor, Second Reformed Church, Pella, IA, and editor at *The Twelve, Perspectives* blog

"This is a marvelous little book of meditations. Schaap – a seventy-year-old American, Protestant, retired college professor – sets his Christian faith next to that of Mother Teresa and discovers that in spite of the vast differences in how they have lived and perceived the Christian life, they 'both share Christ's hand opened lovingly in their lives.' His prose is scintillating, and often playful. (His riff on Mother Teresa's use of the word "bedew" in one of the meditations is a gem.) His insights as he compares his life to hers are personal yet they move toward the universal and are often wise."

David Schelhaas, Emeritus Professor of English, Dordt College, and author of *Illuminated Manuscript* and *The God of Material Things*

READING
MOTHER TERESA

To Mike & Elizabeth

READING
MOTHER TERESA

A Calvinist looks lovingly at
"the little bride of Christ"

James Calvin Schaap

James Calvin Schaap

DORDT COLLEGE PRESS

Printed in the United States of America.

Dordt College Press   www.dordt.edu/DCPcatalog
498 Fourth Avenue NE
Sioux Center, Iowa 51250

ISBN: 978-1-940567-13-6

The Library of Congress Cataloging-in-Publication Data is on file with the Library of Congress, Washington, D.C.
Library of Congress Control Number: 2015957918

Table of Contents

Preface

Last night I had to push myself to go to church, to listen to the still small voice of *should* in order to get dressed and leave the house. I went mostly because I knew that being there would beat the alternative, the guilt of not having gone. Last night going to church was "an exercise in spiritual discipline" – to use the acceptable language of contemporary piety. Sometimes in the chambers of my dark soul, church-going simply relieves guilt. I know that's bad. I don't need a lecture – I came from the factory with a humming Calvinist conscience.

By the time I left the driveway, I was late. The bank clock in town said two minutes to, and I was five minutes away – and church in rural Iowa operates on time. When I pulled up, I figured I'd be last and just grab a seat somewhere in the back where no one would see me anyway – don't make yourself a distraction, that kind of thing.

On the way in, I met a couple, also late; a couple we'd just been talking about at dinner, when my daughter and father-in-law mentioned a terrible accident not all that far from where we live; a fatal crash that had taken the life of a local man, a husband, and a father to four sons.

"We were just talking about you," I told that couple as we hustled up to the front door of church, the organ already playing. "Were you related to the guy who was killed last week?"

"Brother," he said. That's all, and then he stopped and looked at me with the emptied eyes of someone who's not so much lost as dizzy. He's a good man, a strong man, a square-shouldered, broad chested Iowa farmer – and right there on the sidewalk outside of church he held out his hand for me to shake, but also, I think, simply to hold. And why wouldn't he? His brother left last week early Tuesday morning in the twinkling of an eye. The man needed to be touched, needed to be held – we all do – because that brother of his had been there Monday night, like always, and then simply gone, just like that. Gone. And not coming back.

We ended up in the same pew, the three of us, and having them beside me changed everything about worship because it was impossible *not* to hear what I heard, to sing what I sang, to experience what I experienced through the eyes and ears and mind and heart of a man who'd just that week lost a brother.

One of the first hymns, chosen by a teenager, was the prayer of St.

Francis – "Make me a channel of your peace."

I'd been reading a biography of St. Francis, because he and his life and devotion meant so very much to Mother Teresa, who I've also been thinking about – two storied Roman Catholic mystics, a man and woman who, by their profession, actually spoke with God.

It's hard to imagine worlds more distanced – a retired teacher and a grieving farm family on the emerald edge of the Great Plains worshiping in a tightly-bound Calvinist church peopled almost exclusively by Dutch-Americans; an Albanian oath-bound "religious" who gave her life away on the streets of Calcutta, and a goofy, holy fool friar and preacher from 13th century Italy; all of us singing and praying the same words. It was, at least for me, a joyously ecumenical moment.

Mother Teresa was a saint. If I were Catholic, I'd use the present tense, because she is.

To Roman Catholics, she's become one officially, after passing a rigorous investigation that includes her having to have performed documented miracles.

Sometimes I envy the Mother Church for daring to describe some of us as more than creatures of dust. Together, the Catholic saints are a museum of grace that Protestantism – with its stress on individual experience – simply doesn't have. We have Billy Graham and the Reformers, Jonathan Edwards maybe; but we stress immediacy so greatly – me and my God, me and my being born-again, a personal relationship with Jesus Christ – that history, even church history, all too often seems matter-of-fact.

When I picked up *Come Be My Light: The Private Writings of the "Saint of Calcutta"* in the pre-dawn hours of what would be a gorgeous day in the Hill Country of Texas, I was smitten – not only by the story of Mother Teresa's life, about which I knew very little; not only by her unflagging commitment to the poor, which I knew only in outline; not only by her teachings, which I had never heard in her own words; not only by her decades-long dark night of the soul, about which very few of us knew anything; but also by what I shared with her as believer, by what she could teach me, by what I needed to learn, even though my own faith tradition is hopelessly Protestant and even (gulp!) Calvinist. I loved the book, loved the woman whose words fill it.

What struck me immediately was how much alike we are – *and* how different.

In the meditations between the covers of this book, I'm not interested in dissecting orthodox Roman Catholic theology or disparaging sacramentalism. I respect the grand fidelity of the Roman Catholic world. If I were to leave the fellowship of my youth, I'd probably visit the local cathedral far more quickly and often than I would some suburban mega-church.

But the differences also interest me greatly and they are very real. Christianity isn't just spiritual therapy or a political persuasion or even a "worldview." It certainly isn't a place to go for socializing. But it is something of all of those things, as well as a system of thought and a means by which we find ourselves in a world that's a moving target.

The Christian faith is something akin to oxygen, to the air we breathe, to those who share it anyway. It outlines our values and makes pressing demands. By our faith, we determine the shape of things in the world we live. It's organic, alive, capable of acclimating to time and space, and yet principled enough to be an unshakeable foundation, all at once! It helps us determine how to live – and how not to. The Bible, Calvin said, was a pair of spectacles through which we see the world. So is the Christian faith itself.

Still, it accepts immense varieties of human experience and all kinds of people.

Christian believers are different, after all – multi-colored, multi-cultural, multi-ethnic, even multi-valued. I have friends and family, believers all, who are died-in-the-wool political conservatives, and other friends and family, believers all, who roll their eyes at the right-hand side of any political argument. Sometimes Christians are enemies – historically, quite often, in fact.

I have an odd personal history in the American melting pot of American religion. I am – or have been – the child of a single religious tradition, an ethnic denomination that may or may not be on its way to extinction, as are all such ethnic fellowships in the cultural mix we Americans so proudly claim. I am a member of the Christian Reformed Church in North America, have been since birth, as have been my ancestors on both sides of the family. But take it from me, no two of us from the Dutch Reformed family are exactly alike, despite our experience and doctrinal character.

These meditations on the life of Mother Teresa are not intended to bring together, in any way, shape, or form, what broke down during the Reformation. I'm not opposed to such reconciliation, to ecumenicity, but it's helpful to remember that way back when, each of the disciples had his own particular view of who Jesus was and is. Differences exist – and I think they always will.

The meditations that follow are mine; they're what I thought as I read through *Come Be My Light*. What's here is me, and only me.

But maybe they're you too – that's what I'm hoping. My guess is that those who are reading this right now would have sung along heartily last night, all four verses of the prayer of St. Francis. I did, and I know Mother would have, a saint by any profession.

I. The Little Bride of Christ

Do not offer any part of yourself to sin as an instrument of wickedness, but rather offer yourselves to God as those who have been brought from death to life; and offer every part of yourself to him as an instrument of righteousness. Romans 6:13

She calls herself "the little bride of Christ," and even though she was still a child when she used that language, she does so, her letters suggest, with a sense of destiny already in great part fulfilled in her heart and soul – "the little bride of Christ." There had to be thousands like her during her time, all of them – Roman Catholic girls and women – entirely devoted to Jesus, to the virgin mother, and to their special calling as, well, women of the cloth.

Born in Albania, intimately taken with the lives of saints and missionaries, Mother Teresa committed herself early to "the religious life," a phrase that meant to her, a woman and a Roman Catholic, entirely different things, I believe, than it means to me.

A friend of mine once met her in passing, shook her hand, in fact. Someone told her she'd better buy a glove to preserve what she could of the blessed touch of a saint.

I am, as Mother Teresa was, a believer in Jesus Christ; but, at least on the outside, very little of how she described herself is language I can borrow or a tradition I can understand. As a child in an evangelical Christian school, I was taught to revere Luther, Calvin, Knox, and Zwingli, those whose burning righteousness valiantly resisted apostate popish claims. My own heritage is deeply Calvinistic, and even though I was reared 500 years after Calvin, a great number of the Reformation's antagonisms spilled into my consciousness – indulgences, inquisitions, thumb screws, piggish priests growing fat on the poor of the land. Heritage is never quite as pure or sacred as some of us want to believe.

None of the many fine adult Christians I knew as a kid ever asked me – or the little girls in my class – to think of ourselves as "little brides of Christ." That's not my language, our language; it's a metaphor I could never pull over me or feel in my heart. It's hers, and, in part, I believe, the language familiar to a particular time and place that may well be diminishing, if not gone, these days.

I picked up *Mother Teresa: Come Be My Light*[1] on Saturday morning, early, from a bookstore left unlocked at a retreat center in the hill country of Texas. I walked a dozen pages into the book that morning, alone, and was ushered into a story so unlike my own as to be fantasy, yet so much akin that I felt her breath rise from the open page.

I mean no disrespect and have no problems with the canonization of Mother Teresa of Calcutta – hers is a marvelous story, and saints themselves are a venerable tradition. May her thin, angular face, stark and pious, grace a hundred thousand stained glass windows and enrich countless human souls.

That she has much to teach me, and that I have much to learn about being an "instrument of righteousness," doesn't alter the fact that the nature of our shared faith is sometimes greatly different.

Still, we're far more deeply and intimately related than not, the two of us – Mother Teresa of Calcutta and an aging bald male twice her size, recently retired, lugging a Calvinist pedigree, a man who hails from the emerald edge of the Great Plains in the virtual heart of North America.

As children of Adam, we share a mortal coil. We're both undeniably and fully human, and we both know our help is in the name of the Lord, in whose love we draw our every breath.

That is a joy, as I begin to write this morning, a reason for morning thanks.

PRAYER: Lord, make me willing to learn, give me a humble spirit and a willing heart to listen to your story arising from the life of one of your saints. Thank you for the gift of love she gave to the poor of Calcutta and the legacy of commitment she left for all of us who share faith in you, our God. In your son's name, Amen.

---

1   *Mother Teresa: Come Be My Light – The private writings of the "Saint of Calcutta,"* Brian Kolodiejchuk, editor (New York: Image, 2007). Page numbers in parentheses are to this book.

II. Workmanship

"Therefore, whoever takes the lowly position of this child is the greatest in the kingdom of heaven." Matthew 18:4

I was only twelve years old then. It was then that I first knew I had a vocation to the poor . . . in 1922. I wanted to be a missionary, I wanted to go out and give the life of Christ to the people in the missionary countries. . . . (14)

When I was twelve, I got caught stealing cigarettes. When I was twelve, basically I lived across the street from a school playground where one of the three battlefields offered all the joy and thrills I needed – a blacktopped basketball court, hoops sometimes even netted. Caddy-corner was a sandlot baseball field, scraps of cardboard for bases; and enough open space for after-school football, come September. Nary an adult in sight. No uniforms, no score books, no instruction. It was all sandlot. Oh, yeah – and golf midsummer with those wooden clubs we rescued from the trash of a neighbor.

When I was twelve, I went to catechism and church and Christian school. I played piano, poorly, and sang in choirs. I heard the Bible read every time we ate, and listened to my own parents confess their faith openly and lovingly. It seems to me I had every advantage Mother Teresa did spiritually.

I remember writing Elizabeth Elliot after reading *Through Gates of Splendor*, the story of those missionaries murdered by Auca Indians somewhere in South America – and getting a letter back from her, too, a sweet one. It was a school assignment. I was about twelve, I'd say. I remember the book, especially the pictures.

What I don't remember is ever aching to become, someday, a missionary. I just wanted to play ball. Well, and, for a while at least, smoke cigarettes.

I don't think of my childhood as being spiritually or materially impoverished. In fact, I tend to judge it as almost idyllic. Does that make sense?

Maybe what we have to do, saints and sinners alike, is not so much aspire for the holy, the sacred, but learn to look for it, even across the street, where sometimes, strangely enough, it hangs in swaddling tatters from steel hoops on the blacktop.

At twelve I don't think I knew that, but today I believe I do. It was something I had to learn. Maybe Mother Teresa didn't. Maybe she became, even as a child, capable of what Christ extols when he talks, as he often did, about child-like faith.

Honestly, I don't regret my childhood, not even the smokes. I like to rest in the promise that we are, from the cradle, from the womb to the grave, the Lord's own workmanship. What the two of us share, I'm sure – Mother Teresa and me – is his hand opened lovingly in our lives.

PRAYER: Lord, not one of us is the same. We come in different shades and temperaments and shoe sizes. Some recognize as children what they will become, some search forever. Give us peace with what you've given us to become. Shape us all for servanthood, as you do, in a thousand different ways. Amen.

III. Saving Souls

"You snakes! You brood of vipers! How will you escape being condemned to hell?" Matthew 23:33

From the age of 5½ years, – when I first received Him [in Holy Communion] – the love for souls has been within. – It grew with the years – until I came to India – with the hope of saving many souls. (58)

For reasons that I don't understand myself, when it comes to the fires of hell, I have, since childhood, become significantly less fearful. What's more, I'm probably a good deal more generous about who might or might not go there – and why. I am, without question, far more theologically liberal today, maybe even something of a backslider, especially when it comes to hell. My guess is that, for the most part, I'm not alone.

Mother's Teresa's white-hot, childhood passion for "saving many souls" probably arises from a cosmos she saw clearly before her at that age, a cosmos I think I know too, because when I was a kid I saw just two roads leading toward eternity – one wide, one narrow, both clearly and vividly mapped.

I think I knew exactly how to travel down the road to either destination, and it wasn't all that difficult. In my kid-sized mind, salvation had very little to do with the mysteries and miracles of grace, and much more to do with toeing the line in every which way – "oh, be careful little eyes what you see." The "straight-and-narrow" was, for me at least, wholly as understandable, the signage as unmistakable as it is on the interstate to hell.

And hell, for me, was as real as, say, Milwaukee.

If you love people, as Mother Teresa did, you want to save them, at all cost, from the nightmarish visions of Hieronymus Bosch or whatever horror one's mind creates down there at the luminous end of that diabolical road, the wide one. I understand that. She says she was 5½ when she partook of her first communion, just 5½ when those lifelong passions took root. She was a child. She saw things as a child.

Me? – when I became a man, I think I put away those childish things.

Or did I?

Christ's admonitions about babes in arms, about children, about kids, about the dire necessity of simple, untrammeled childhood faith – he was kidding about that, right? Throughout his ministry, he was given to hyperbole, after all – like rich men passing through a needle's eye. How nonsensical is that? – it's poetry, not hard-and-fast truth.

Isn't it?

Besides, what she's talking about here isn't Hieronymus Bosch. What she's talking about is saving souls, her love for them, a full dose of which I think even this learned professor could use.

I'm not as sure as she was at that age, or at this. Nor am I as sure of what "saving souls" really means.

Oddly enough, that having been said, I honestly don't think we're that much different.

PRAYER: Lord grant me, grant us all, a greater love for souls. Help us learn to love others as you would have us do. Fill us with your grace so we can't help but overflow with the glorious excess of your love. Make us your servants. In Jesus' name, Amen.

IV. Purity in Pain

> . . . I consider everything a loss because of the surpassing worth of knowing Christ Jesus my Lord, for whose sake I have lost all things. I consider them garbage, that I may gain Christ. . . . Philippians 3:8

> Fine and pure as summer dew
> Her soft warm tears begin to flow,
> Sealing and sanctifying now
> Her painful sacrifice. (17)

Just before the epic battle that would forever change Native American life on the Great Plains, the Battle at Greasy Grass, or Little Big Horn, Sitting Bull, a Lakota medicine man, performed a Sun Dance, then cut chunks of his own flesh from his arms and legs as an act of devotion to the divine, or the sacred, *Wakan Tanka*. Bloodied and weakened, he then saw a vision of cavalrymen falling from the sky. That vision, historians say, both red and white, strengthened Native resolve for the battle that was to come.

Sitting Bull (1831–1890)

Barbaric. Heathenish. Sure. But somehow, to a religious person, understandable. What Sitting Bull did that day was a sacrifice. He gave bloodily of himself to his god, humbled himself, hurt himself in contrition and submission to his own image of the divine.

Mother Teresa was little more than a child, really, when, tears in her eyes, she wrote a self-reflective poem on her trip to India, a poem that describes her mood on board that ship. I believe her when she says she cried. I believe her tears. She had to be anxious about the world she was entering and what was to come. She was little more than a college freshman away from home for the first time, I've seen them cry in torrents.

What's difficult for me to understand is that she considered the way she had pledged herself to God and his love to be such an immense sacrifice. If she truly valued what she might have become had she *not* chosen to take her orders, being on that ship and on her way to a whole new life would have been more difficult, and much less filled with the sweet promise that she was soon to become, after all, "the little bride of Christ"?

Yet, here, in the last lines of that little poem, she says her tears, "pure as the summer dew," flowed from her "painful sacrifice."

I don't think Mother Teresa ever pulled out some kind of poetic license to wrench out half-truths or hyperbole. I can see her there on the deck of that ship, little more than a kid, handkerchief in hand, dabbing at her eyes.

What I don't understand is her *sacrifice*.

But then, I just returned from the gym, where I work out lest my weight balloon, as it certainly could. Our house is comfy and warm. Sometime this week, I'm getting a new easy chair. Tuesdays and Wednesdays are tough teaching days for me, but I'm sure I'll come out whole on the other side. I haven't cut out any chunks of my flesh as of late, haven't worn the hooks in a Sun Dance, haven't denied myself anything to speak of, haven't even fasted. I just don't think I've done much suffering.

With so much of her storied life still in front of her, so much suffering yet to be discovered and endured, so much love yet to be given away, it's difficult for me to understand how tears could possibly be wrenched from what this young lady, still a child, thought of as her significant sacrifice in following Jesus.

But then, maybe that's my fault. Not long ago, we sang the old hymn "I Surrender All." Really? I do?

Maybe I don't recognize her sacrifice because I haven't a clue about my own.

Maybe.

PRAYER: Lord, help us to understand sacrifice. Help us to understand giving. Help us to understand suffering, really, for your sake. Bring us closer to you. Amen.

V. Holy Fool

"I remember the devotion of your youth, how as a bride you loved me and followed me through the desert, through a land not sown."
Jeremiah 2:2

She was just 19 years old when, after six-weeks aboard a passenger ship, she started up the River Ganges, the "Holy River," into Bengal, and met, along with the others, her "Indian sisters." Then, in the convent chapel, together, she says, they "thanked our dear Saviour for this great grace that He had so safely brought us to the goal for which we had been longing" (17).

To her friends and family back home, she wrote, "Pray much for us that we may be good and courageous missionaries" (17).

Sister Teresa was only 19 years old, no different from the students in the chairs in my own classrooms, the very ones who text their friends the moment they shut their books; but she was ready to give her life away as a missionary for our Lord. At that moment, she had to be filled with equal measures of fear and conviction. She had to be, at that moment, near unto God. What she could not have known was how near.

She thought she knew what she would be – "a good and courageous missionary." But in reality she knew next to nothing of what she would become, even less about the squalid world she was about to discover, a world overflowing with the desperation of children she would touch.

At that moment, her youth, idealism, and blind faith carried her triumphantly into a fray she didn't know was there. She could have had no clue that her selflessness, her righteous dedication to the poor of Calcutta would, in time, establish for her a place among the most revered saints of this world. She had little more than a child's sense of what God almighty had in store for her. Really, she knew nothing at all.

In this complex world of ours, naïveté can sometimes prove a blessing. A young church down the block is filled with the Spirit these days, sure as anything that they've embarked on a crusade that is like none other in the community. They're going to do things right; as a fellowship, they're not going to be overrun by tradition or the way it's always been. They're the new Reformation.

It's not rhetoric. It's a mission they believe.

I'm older and tons less sure.

But there's something to be said about child-like dreams, of innocence and daring, something to be envied in a real holy fool.

Sister Teresa's bravado as she begins her ministry, given what little she really knew of what was to come, is downright astounding. But even more amazing is the grace that crowned her, even as a girl.

PRAYER: It is, dear Lord, far easier to have convictions than to act on them. Give us clarity of vision and the determination to be your hands in this world. Help us to care and to love as unceasingly as you do. Give us a simple heart for others. Amen.

VI. Beginnings

Satisfy us in the morning with your unfailing love, that we may sing for joy and be glad all our days. Psalm 90:14

According to the *Wall Street Journal* of May 25, 1931, Treasury Secretary Mellon advised that the Hoover Administration was saying no to a tax increase, which was not to say, he asserted, that some kind of increase was definitely and finally off the table. Should they determine to hike taxes, the Treasury Department, he said, would seek broadening the tax base rather than simply raising rates. After all, only 2.5 million individuals out of a 120 million population pay income taxes, and 380,000 of those pay about 97 percent.

On May 25, 1931, *The Wall Street Journal* reported that the Investment Bankers Association of America listened to proposals designed to safeguard US investors when obtaining foreign securities because present conditions for such investments were bound to prolong economic depression.

On May 25, 1931, an editorial in the *WSJ* noted misleading coverage of the Supreme Court reversing a decision in the case of Yetta Stromberg, who'd been convicted under California's "Red Flag" law for displaying a "red flag, banner, badge, or device of any color . . . as a sign of . . . opposition to organized government." The court, the editorial argued, had left in place provisions against anarchy and sedition.

The *Wall Street Journal* of May 25, 1931 contains no mention of a young lady in India, Sister Teresa, making the first profession of her vows after two years of her novitiate training, vows that promised a life of "poverty, charity, and obedience" (18).

"If you could know how happy I am, as Jesus' little spouse," she wrote a friend. "No one, not even those who are enjoying some happiness which in the world seems perfect, could I envy, because I am enjoying my complete happiness, even when I suffer something for my beloved Spouse" (18).

I rather doubt her first profession was noted anywhere in the English-speaking world. Why should it have been?

Nothing the *Wall Street Journal* said that day was miniscule or incidental. Significant events were occurring, the country smack-dab in the middle of something people only later would call "The Great Depression." I'm sure the newsroom buzzed that day, breathed a collective sigh of relief once the first edition was out.

But on the other side of the world a young woman was taking her vows before God, vows that would lead to a lifelong profession of faith eventually witnessed by most of the world.

Other than a few who witnessed the event, no one wrote up the story.

Somehow, that it wasn't seems a blessing.

PRAYER: We are creatures of time, Lord, but you are God of all eternity. Help us measure our joy and our successes in ways that honor your eternity – and not just our time. Teach us to number our days. Amen.

VII. To Teach All Nations

"Go into all the world and preach the good news to all creation."
Mark 16:15

From May of 1931 until 1948, Sister Teresa taught Indian children at St. Mary's Bengali Medium School for girls.

Now I'll admit to a decidedly draconian view of childhood education in Catholic schools in the early years of the 20th century, here in the States that is. Jowly nuns nearly bursting out of their straitjacket habits rule medieval classrooms by thumb-screws and other unthinkable persuasions.

I don't know where those images come from – perhaps from my own Protestant (which is to say, anti-Catholic) boyhood. But maybe Louise Erdrich is to blame; the nuns in her novels reach out from between the covers and author evil in your own worst dreams.

Somehow it's hard for me to think of little Sister Teresa, this diminutive young lady, barely more than a child, holding forth before an overcrowded classroom of little girls and being anything less than cherubic. Honestly, she couldn't be draconian if she tried, right?

Who knows what little Sister Teresa might have been like as a teacher? Eventually the world came to esteem her greatly, not for creative lesson plans or cool classroom tricks, but because of her sacrificial rescue work among the world's poorest and often abandoned little ones. Later on in her life, she wasn't teaching multiplication tables, she was simply keeping otherwise wasted children alive.

But in her starchy black habit she stood before 17 successive classrooms of poor Indian children. We know how she saw her calling – or at least we know how she wanted others to think about how she saw her calling, her work. This is what she wrote to a Catholic magazine back home:

> The heat of India is simply burning. When I walk around, it seems to me that fire is under my feet from which even my body is burning. When it is hardest, I console myself with the thought that souls are saved in this way and that dear Jesus suffered much more for them. . . . (18–19)

Wasn't easy.

And then she goes on, in a very general way, to describe her classroom in terms any teacher will understand. "The life of a missionary is not strewn with roses," she says, "in fact more with thorns. . ." (19). Aha. Short attention spans likely annoyed her, as did vagrant eyes and minds, belligerence and boredom in her students. Most teachers feel such things at some time or another. I did. She had to know children whose out-of-the-classroom problems loomed so terribly before them that they simply couldn't sit.

Think of her this way – she wiped noses, buttoned buttons, slapped hands that reached where they shouldn't have. I bet she read more than her share of lousy assignments. Kids likely tangled in her class, hazed each other, made each other cry.

"[B]ut with it all," she writes somewhat generically, "it is a life full of happiness and joy when she thinks that she is doing the same work which Jesus was doing when He was on earth, and that she is fulfilling Jesus' commandment: 'Go and teach all nations!'" (19).

Funny, even after forty years in the classroom, I always thought Jesus' departing command was not to teach but to preach. But then, I'm Protestant, and I'm not a woman whose vows to be the bride of Christ gave her a very clear and cozy sense of mission in the classroom.

Maybe I've been wrong. No matter. Even though I've been a teacher for forty years, I can still learn.

And Mother Teresa, long after she quit and long after she died, can still teach.

All nations, too.

PRAYER: Lord, give us all a sense of mission, make us all missionaries and teachers. Equip each of us to go into all the world and teach the nations – with computers, mechanical hammers, food processors, and whiteboards, with power points, with our weaving and silversmithing, with everything we do and say. Bless all of us who confess with your name in the sacred office of teacher, even those who never enter a classroom. Establish the work of our hands, Lord – establish the work of our hands. Amen.

VIII. Perpetual Vows

"Where you die I will die, and there I will be buried. May the Lord deal with me, be it ever so severely, if even death separates you and me." Ruth 1:17

Hamlet – Act I, scene 1. Hamlet's father's ghost appears, speaks only to his son, tells him how his Uncle Claudius, now on the throne and in "the incestuous sheets" of Hamlet's mother's bed, murdered him, Hamlet's own father, the former King. He then spurs on Hamlet to revenge. "Swear!" he moans, as if the fires of hell were already at his ankles. "Swear! Swear! Swear!"

On the first day we discussed the play, a student raised his hand. "They must have taken oaths really seriously in those days," he said.

The subtext is obvious: the student figured that today, generally, people don't. He may be right.

"Very seriously," I told him. We didn't talk about today.

Yesterday, in church, a young lady stood up and answered three questions and thereby underwent a liturgical ritual we call "Profession of Faith." I listened to the questions, read them closely, far closer, I imagine, than I did when, almost 50 years ago, those same questions were read to me. Back then, I, for one, didn't take an oath all that seriously.

That's the life experience I bring to Sister Teresa's oath, her "profession of perpetual vows," on May 25, 1931, after two years of initiation into the world she was entering, her novitiate, promising a life of poverty, chastity, and obedience. Hers, unlike mine, is much closer to that of Ruth, to her mother-in-law, Naomi. Sister Teresa's vows were a heartfelt dedication built on generations of Roman Catholic tradition, an emphatic personal dedication, as pure as it was resolute. "Before crosses used to frighten me," she wrote to her spiritual guide, "I used to get goose bumps at the thought of suffering – but now I embrace suffering even before it actually comes, and like this Jesus and I live in love" (20).

Yesterday, in that young lady's home, where her profession of faith I'm sure was certainly celebrated, her mom and dad threw a great party, thrilled even to the soul at what their daughter committed herself to in our public worship.

It's altogether possible that Sister Teresa listened to voices more akin to Hamlet's father's bellowing at his reluctant son, and it goes without saying that she took her "profession of perpetual vows" vastly more seriously than I did, years ago, when I stood before a congregation of worshippers and professed my faith publicly. But neither yesterday's young lady, nor Sister Teresa, nor me – nor anyone else, for that matter – no matter how seriously we take our oaths, is ever going to believe that what was said, what was sworn to, even in the presence of many others, will be some kind of spiritual shield against woe in this vale of tears. It won't. It couldn't have been, and it hasn't been.

Still, I hear that ghost. "Swear!" he told his son. Heard him just yesterday again, in fact. Once upon a time, a young Albanian school teacher, in the soaring heat of New Delhi, India, listened to a voice asking her for commitment. And she too swore.

And when she did, all the ghosts, I'd like to think, went joyfully silent.

PRAYER: Lord, give us the strength and the grace to let our ayes be ayes and our nays be nays. Help us to live in truth, your truth. Amen.

IX. Prayer as Work – Work as Prayer

"Commit to the Lord whatever you do. . . ." Proverbs 16:3

"But one thing I beg of you: pray always for me. For that you do not need special time – because our work is our prayer. . . ." (21)

LuAnn Arceneaux makes several appearances in Andre Dubus' final book of short stories, *Dancing after Hours*, but perhaps her most memorable is in "Out of the Snow," when, armed only with instinct, guts, and a frying pan, she dispatches two would-be rapists who follow her home from the market.

LuAnn's marriage is not without its scary moments, but her life and that of her husband, outlined in the stories, grow slowly stronger, as does their commitment, in part because of LuAnn's maturing Roman Catholic faith. Dubus, who died some time ago, was a practicing Catholic, but no saint – for sure, no saint. His son, Andre Dubus III, makes that very clear in his memoir, *Townie*.

No matter, Dubus the elder's story "Out of the Snow" is a memorable gift of grace. Before the astounding pasting she puts on the creeps who tail her home, LuAnn tells her husband that she has begun to understand that "she must be five again" to be "like Saint Therese of Lisieux, who knew at a very young age that the essence of life was to be found in the simplest of tasks."

At breakfast, LuAnn sees her work as sacrament:

Watching the brown sugar bubbling in the light of the flames, smelling it and the cinnamon, and listening to her family talking about snow, she told herself that this toast and oatmeal were a sacrament, the physical form that love assumed in this moment, as last night's lovemaking was, as most of her actions were. When she was able to remember this and concentrate on it, she knew the significance of what she was doing; as now, using a pot holder, she drew the pan from the oven, then spooned the oatmeal into bowls her family came from the dining room to receive from her hands.

That's the frying pan she will wield to rout her bozo attackers just a few hours later.

LuAnn's quest to see her work and life as sacrament is, I believe, what Mother Teresa means when she tells her former confessor in a letter that she needs his prayers, but that he needn't spend any special time praying "because our work is our prayer." Later, she would tell others, "Work is not prayer; prayer is not work, but we must pray the work for Him, with Him and to Him" (364).

I wish I were adept at doing that. I wish it were easier. I wish my eyes were open to see a frying pan as a means of grace, because Mother Teresa isn't wrong. Seeing our lives as holy makes all the difference, whether or not our would-be attackers are routed.

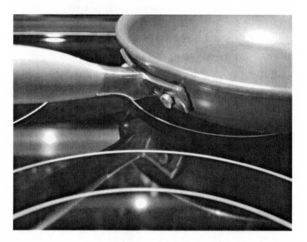

This morning, I'm thankful for LuAnn Arceneaux and Mother Teresa for pointing so enduringly at the true blessing of nothing less than grace itself, grace not simply in the beyond, but in the here and now, in the dust in which we live, in the dust of which we are.

PRAYER: There are these moments, Lord, when the chasm between you and what we do seems too far too wide to bridge. Help us find you in the everyday tasks of our lives. Give us grace to see your grace in everything in this your world. Amen.

X. Do Bedew

But now in Christ Jesus you who once were far away have been brought near by the blood of Christ. Ephesians 2:13

India is as scorching as is hell – but its souls are beautiful and precious because the Blood of Christ has bedewed them. (21)

I've never before in my life seen the word *bedewed*. In some ways, the sound of the word itself is a hoot, easily mistaken for the patter of some late-50s crooner. The word makes all kinds of sense, of course, an arranged marriage between *be* and *do*, words that are already almost kissing cousins, never comingled quite as intimately as they are here: *bedewed*.

Mother Teresa wasn't making it up either. I looked. *Bedewed* is perfectly legitimate and available for use, free of charge; but I don't know I've ever, ever seen it or heard it before. Well, maybe. Hum the theme from the Pink Panther movies sometime, and you'll hear it – "Be-dew, bedew, bedew-bedew-bedew, bedew, bedewwwwwwwwwwwwwwwwwwwwwwwwww, bedew be dew."

Something like that.

It's just a goofy word, or is that just my imagination? – *bedewed*, the kind of word you could drop into the bin full of synonyms for drunk, as in, "Good Lord, I got myself totally bedewed Saturday."

Mother Teresa is creating a double metaphor too, which is sometimes more than a little risky. It's one thing to say that the heat-tortured poor of India are wet with, refreshed by, and even kept from death by dew, but that which really coats and cools them isn't dew at all – it's blood, Christ's own. Now some who are unfamiliar with the blood atonement might call that creepy, but Mother Teresa certainly didn't make it up. The heat – which was substantial, I'm sure – is not India's but hell's, at least I think that's the implication. The whole line is heavy-laden with metaphor because if there was blood on the streets of Calcutta, my guess is it was theirs, the people's, not Christ's. Unless you're Catholic. Of course, that's not meant literally. Or is it, sacramentally? By the greatest miracle of all, she says, Christ's own blood, given for us and for them, keeps them – and us – *bedewed*.

I like it – *bedewed*, I mean. The word makes me smile because it's goofy and twisted and not meant the way it's said at all, and yet it is. In the middle of a sometimes scorched world, Christ's love forever keeps bedewing us. That's right, bedewing us! – as in, bedew, bedew, bedew.

You can sing that. I bet you can.

This morning, after some powerful storms, the fog is so thick that the end of the world seems a block away. We live and move and have our being in an odd flat gray room. Last night's storms brewed up a tornado that swept through a small town not all that far away.

There, things are wet this morning, I'm sure. Amid all the debris, no one is sweltering and few of the homeless are dry. Rains came heavily before and after the twister. There's no one dead, but when all those people walk out onto Main Street and look at the destruction, and when those residents who are now homeless survey the damage, I hope, they too, are blessedly bedewed.

Bedew them, Lord – bedew, bedew, bedew.

PRAYER: Bedew us, Lord, bless us with your grace, wash us all with your blood, drench us with your divine will, your power and glory each morning of each day. Amen.

XI. The Companion of Darkness

How long, Lord? Will you forget me forever? How long will you hide your face from me? How long must I wrestle with my thoughts and day after day have sorrow in my heart? How long will my enemy triumph over me?

Look on me and answer, Lord my God. Give light to my eyes, or I will sleep in death, and my enemy will say, "I have overcome him," and my foes will rejoice when I fall. Psalm 13:1–4

I would like to believe that the two are not somehow related. I would like *not* to believe that the height my faith can reach is somehow conversely proportional to, a backwards mirror image of, the depths to which it can fall or fail.

In Mother Teresa's case, however, it seems sadly true.

My mother told me that my father told her in one of those late-night talks all good marrieds have that he had never once in his life ever doubted that God was there with him, that Jesus was everything his Word said he was and is, and that God loved him truly – my father. We chose "Blessed Assurance" at his funeral because each of his children knew perfectly well that what that old hymn claims was true of our loving father.

I don't look like my father. I'm almost a head taller and probably uncomfortably close to a 100 pounds heavier. I certainly don't see the world the way he did. He was a rock-solid conservative Republican. My father was a wise investor and a hard-worker, and he simply assumed that everyone else should be too. The two of us got along just warmly, but we often disagreed. He was not disagreeable, however. Never.

I like to think I might have inherited at least a bit of his abounding graciousness, even if he and I didn't protect the political turf he did so aggressively. About that, however, I'm a lousy judge. I also like to believe his greatest gift to his only son was faith that ambles through life like the Eveready bunny, somehow protected from the energy failure that creates bouts in some of us of horrific, crippling doubt.

Mother Teresa was not so blessed, a fact of her life that some, I'm sure, would much rather not stumble upon. The same letter that "bedews" Indian souls contains the first mention of the darkness to which she was more than occasionally subject throughout her life. "Do not think my life is strewn with roses," she writes, "that is the flower which I hardly ever find on my way. . . . I have more often as my companion 'darkness'" (20).

The heights to which her faith and her spirits could climb had to be incredible; but somehow I'm not surprised that when she would fall, that descent would take her into darkness deeper and more profound than most of us will ever see.

It's really hard to think of this tiny little saint suffering that way, to think of anyone suffering that way; but it's comforting too to know that we all suffer, that Psalm 13 isn't just David on a bad day, or Psalm 88 isn't the ravings of an infidel.

Even though I swear I've not been there, not been to the darkness Mother Teresa knew too well, my own unquestioned faith is richer, deeper, and fuller by way of her testimony that she was. I don't want to sound vainglorious, but I think I am made stronger by way of her weakness.

It saddens me to know that somehow this little bride of Christ suffered the profound doubt that grows from a perception of abandonment by the almighty. Yet, somehow her darkness – and her testimony about it, just like that of King David – brings me light.

PRAYER: Many of us thank you, Lord, for Mother Teresa's testimony – her saintliness, her courage, the unending fountain of her love for the poorest of the poor. But thank you too for the testimony of human darkness in the hours of her loving service. Thank you for the testimony of her humanness because it helps us know ours. Amen.

XII. Nothing Out of the Ordinary

"For I was hungry and you gave me something to eat. . . ." Matthew 25:35

Greta Garbo is there, as is Ray Milland, Deanna Durbin, and, of course, the Dutch Royal Family. I've been to the Annex twice, and was struck both times by the ordinariness of it all, the room's walls festooned with pix of famous people who drew her fancy.

You stand there in that little room and you say to yourself that the young lady who stuck these pictures on her bedroom walls, Anne Frank, was not a whit different from any other young lady really except she was Jewish in occupied Holland in the middle of the Second World War. But because she wrote down what she was feeling and experiencing, she left a testimony treasured by millions.

Anne Frank

I thought of Anne Frank when I read this line from *Come Be My Light*: ". . . there was nothing so out of the ordinary about her as to attract the attention of the archbishop or anyone else" (23).

Sister Teresa became Mother Teresa on May 24, 1937, after taking her final vows in the convent chapel at Darjeeling. Had you or I been there, there would have been nothing at all to catch our attention because she wouldn't have distinguished herself in the least from those others who took vows with her. We wouldn't have recognized her as someone who would become what she became. She was, right then, uniquely ordinary.

In an odd way, her ordinariness harmonizes with these words from Matthew 25, the only place in the gospels where Jesus talks much about the afterlife, where he speaks specifically about sheep and goats and the two starkly different directions people will take at judgment.

> "Then the King will say to those on his right, 'Come, you who are blessed by my Father; take your inheritance, the kingdom prepared

for you since the creation of the world. For I was hungry and you gave me something to eat, I was thirsty and you gave me something to drink, I was a stranger and you invited me in, I needed clothes and you clothed me, I was sick and you looked after me, I was in prison and you came to visit me.'"

What follows is one of the strangest verses in scripture, methinks, because even the righteous – even those who obeyed and paid attention, who gave mercy and clothed the naked, visited the prisoners, brought food to the hungry – even those have no clue:

"Then the righteous will answer him, 'Lord, when did we see you hungry and feed you, or thirsty and give you something to drink? When did we see you a stranger and invite you in, or needing clothes and clothe you? When did we see you sick or in prison and go to visit you?'"

The righteous, no different from the condemned, had no clue about their own blessed work. They were blind to the fact they'd allowed themselves to become the hands of Christ. Whatever they did, they did thoughtlessly, exercising an almost instinctive righteous propensity to lend a hand. They were needed and they helped. Not even a comma there.

In 1944, standing in her room, no one could have guessed that Anne Frank would tell a story that has featured the Holocaust more fully than almost any other. No one could have predicted what she scribbled down would become one of the world's great books. But then, eight years earlier, no one could have guessed that a diminutive Albanian woman, the newly named Mother Teresa, would become *the* Mother Teresa.

She was no prodigy, nor was she somehow marked for greatness. She was simply someone who let herself be used, someone who saw hungry people and tried with every bit of her heart, soul, and mind to find ways to feed them, to give them his love with hers.

There are mysteries in our lives that go beyond, far beyond, our ken. But not his.

PRAYER: Just like Mary, mother of Jesus, a woman she adored, Mother Teresa seems to arise out of nowhere, a woman you chose, Lord, not because she in any way distinguished herself as a child or even as a young adult. You took her and made her be yours to give your love away. Use us, Lord. Shape us divinely into your servants. Amen.

XIII. To Laugh

"Surely God does not reject one who is blameless or strengthen the hands of evildoers. He will yet fill your mouth with laughter and your lips with shouts of joy." Job 8:20–21

Sister Gabriela is here. She works beautifully for Jesus – the most important is that she knows how to suffer and at the same time how to laugh. That is the most important – to suffer and to laugh. (24)

Up beside my office desk there stands a picture of the Reverend Bernard J. Haan, founder and first president of the college where I taught for the last 37 years. It's almost 70 years old, from *Life* magazine, in fact; he's outfitted in his finest swallow-tail coat, holding forth in front of the pipe organ, no pulpit in sight.

It has to be posed because I can't imagine that a professional photographer – some worldly guy from *Time* or *Life* – would have been allowed to wander up the aisle during Sunday worship to shoot, willy-nilly, umpteen photographs of the Dominie opening the Word of the Lord. Wouldn't have happened.

"I'd like to have a picture of you holding forth," the New Yorker would have said some weekday morning, and the fiery young preacher reached for that swallow-tail coat.

I didn't know him when he was a young preacher, but I've heard enough about him to be able to guess that he hammered that pulpit, beat out his strongest points on the massive Bible that sat up there back then. He was young, robust, opinionated, and charismatic. Within a few years, he had accumulated a following so wide that he'd had sufficient deep-pocketed disciples to start a college, part of that following growing from a reputation he gained for keeping a theater out of the small Iowa town where he lived – the reason *Time* and *Life* were in town back then.

A couple of decades later, by the mid-60s, he was a warm and genial old codger, capable of measured self-reflection, a fiery preacher who could – and did, famously – laugh at himself.

By the time he retired, he could actually "do" himself in legendary self-parody. He knew what the crowd expected of him, that he could play himself – with style and grace. And success.

Late in life, he told me that when he looked back, he wished it hadn't taken him so long to learn that the way to the human heart is via a smile, a laugh, some sweet joy. That's what he told me. He regretted not learning that lesson earlier. I keep that old picture of him around because it helps me remember what he says it took so long for him to learn.

I don't know that the Rev. B. J. Haan suffered – or how, but I'm confident all of us do. And I don't know about Mother Teresa's friend Gabriela either – how she might have suffered there on the streets of Calcutta. I can't compare her suffering with his; but then, really, it's impossible ever to match my suffering up against yours or anyone else's. Suffering is suffering.

But I think Mother Teresa wasn't wrong about laughter. Not to smile is to suffer ceaselessly. There is something like grace in what she says here – "the most important" is to suffer *and* to laugh.

Down at the bottom of that assessment is paradox: laughter without suffering is silliness; suffering without laughter is horror. Life is a prickly dance between the two, a balancing act.

I was young when B. J. told me about his regrets, young enough to remember what he advised: To laugh, a tough lesson, he said, smiling.

PRAYER: Help us to laugh, Lord – help us to find joy in the antics of this world – in the flowers and critters, in each other, in ourselves. Give us merriment and joy in your own unfailing love, your generous grace, your bountiful companionship all the days of our lives. Amen.

XIV. Blessed Suffering

Praise our God, O peoples, let the sound of his praise be heard;
> he has preserved our lives and kept our feet from slipping.
For you, O God, tested us; you refined us like silver.
You brought us into prison and laid burdens on our backs.
You let men ride over our heads; we went through fire and water,
> but you brought us to a place of abundance. Psalm 66:8–12

Sister Bernard is making her vows on 23rd January 1938. Thanks be to God now again everything is all right – Jesus has surely chosen her for something special, since He has given her so much suffering. And she is a real hero, bearing up everything courageously with a smile. . . . (24)

Not long ago, in a little privately-printed history of a small town church, I ran through the list of servicemen and discovered the stories of two men, same last name, both pilots, both killed, one in World War II, the other in the Korean War. I mentioned that in a speech I gave in that very small-town church.

Afterward a man came up to me to tell me there was more. "They were brothers," he said.

The history had not mentioned that.

"And you want to know what else?" he asked. "Their mother lost her husband in the First War."

It's the kind of story that must be told to be believed. A woman marries, sometime before 1917. Her husband goes off to "the war to end all wars" and, with thousands of other doughboys, doesn't return. I can only imagine the heartbreak.

Someone else comes along – some local farmer maybe – and marries this young widow. Together they have children, including two boys. In 1942, one of them goes off to military service, becomes a pilot, then is killed, shot down over Europe. I can only imagine the heartbreak.

Another son enlists when America goes to war in Korea. He too becomes a pilot – what an honor. But he too gets shot down and doesn't return.

Who, really, can imagine the heartbreak?

There's a syllogism at work here in Mother Teresa's assessment that's worth examining, and it goes like this: *major premise*: to be blessed means to suffer; *minor premise*: Sister Bernard suffers greatly; *conclusion*: Sister Bernard is blessed.

I have no idea who Sister Bernard is, but neither do I doubt that Sister Bernard – or Mother Teresa for that matter – suffered greatly. Still, I don't know what to make of the logic – "you're blessed if you suffer."

Perhaps I'm skeptical because the logic gets easily manipulated. Some politicians curry favor with their loyal followers because they suffer, they say, at the hands of the media: "see my suffering? – I must be worth your vote." I don't know if I buy the syllogism, even if Mother Teresa is the one bringing it up.

But then, maybe I'm plumb full of guilt. For the last week it's been high-nineties, a swampish gooey heat that rolls sweat down into my neck when I do nothing more than turn brats on the grill. But we've got an air-conditioned house. We eat like kings and queens. Right now, in our fridge, there's sun tea, lemonade, some exotic beer from a micro-brewery, two gallons of cold milk, and ice cubes spewing forever from the freezer's front door. We're not suffering.

I'm not at all sure I have ever suffered, at least not like that woman who once upon a time lost a husband and then, in two subsequent wars, two sons. Last week's toll in our church's "joys and concerns" was staggering. People are suffering – people I know. All kinds of cancers seem to be everywhere. This vale of tears is not without its great and heavy sadnesses.

But are those who suffer somehow blessed for their suffering?

Here's the only truth I think I know. God almighty wants us, always, on our knees, and somehow – I wish it weren't true – it's just plain easier to be on your knees when you can't stand up. Sometimes he puts us there – me too – because maybe it's easier to see him when, like a penitent, the only thing before our eyes is the basement floor.

When there's nowhere else to turn, you can only look up.

PRAYER: No one likes being on his or her knees, Lord. It's not the most comfortable position for most of us. But we understand that you put us there sometimes because otherwise we might too easily forget that you are God and we aren't. Put us on our knees, Lord, and take our hands and lift us up. Amen.

XV. TOTAL DEPRAVITY

We all, like sheep, have gone astray, each of us has turned to our own way. . . . Isaiah 53:6

I should, I suppose, consult some dog-eared, learned treatise. I need to walk only two blocks to find a fine theological library. Shoot, today, who needs a library? – I could simply google "total depravity." It would not be difficult for me to learn more about what those two words mean. What I know about "total depravity," the T, the first letter of the famous Calvinist acronym T-U-L-I-P, is what I've picked up about it through the years.

I don't know what the great theologians speculate about the nature of our human misery, post-Fall. I should check. Undoubtedly, there's more than one opinion.

What I do know is what my own human experience tells me, and it's not exactly what my graduate school advisor used to claim. "Jim, I want you to know that I'm a Calvinist too, just not a Christian," he'd say. "When I look at the world, all I see is crap."

I don't think that "total depravity" means that human beings are pigs. My old advisor was great guy, and I liked him a ton; but his aim was off by more than a few yards.

I think Mother Teresa has it down. Listen to this, from a letter to a mentor: "One thing, pray much for me – I need prayer more than ever," she writes. "I want to be only all for Jesus – truly and not only in name or dress." The year is 1937. The place is Calcutta. Undoubtedly, she wore the habit. "Many times this goes upside-down" – *this* idea of being only all for Jesus – "so my most reverend 'I' gets the most important place. Always the same proud Gonda" (25).

The very idea of this most righteous woman, this woman who has given her life for the poor and destitute, given up everything, the idea of Mother Teresa herself going to war with pride is remarkable, isn't it? Almost beyond belief.

But then, we have her words. Every day, every moment, in the caverns of her own soul she fought an infernal holy war.

Yesterday I finished a story, and I was proud of it – proud because it took a ton of work and I thought I'd pulled it off. I liked it, believed it was good. It was hard, frickin' work, and it took me too many days to accomplish; but the joy of creativity is to gather together stuff – an idea, an anecdote or two, a taste of character, an odd event, a few good names, a hillside, some sheep – and then, like a creator, somehow roll it up together and have it somehow make sense. Art, I think, is little more than finding order in chaos.

I was proud of myself in a good sense. I'd made something that I thought was good and new and wonderful. That kind of pride is no sin. That kind of pride has little to do with total depravity.

But the moment I think I need to be praised is the moment "the most reverend 'I'" struts in, dressed in impish finery. The moment I want acclaim is the moment *my* needs, *my* wants, *my* desires overshadow anything else. And it happens. Always. Total depravity, at least in my experience, is the sad human condition of "me first."

I don't think I'm alone. Mother Teresa's "most reverend 'I'" would not stay in the closet, she says.

We all need prayer. We all need grace. Even Mother Teresa. Depravity is that total.

PRAYER: Perhaps our most monumental struggle – at least for some of us – is the war we maintain with pride – separating our will from that of yours, Lord. Give us the strength and grace to deny ourselves, even when, humanly, it seems we're powerless against thinking of ourselves first. Forgive us and bless us with a love that will teach us something about grace. Amen.

XVI. Paradox

Blessed are the meek, for they will inherit the earth.
Blessed are those who hunger and thirst for righteousness,
    for they will be filled.
Blessed are the merciful, for they will be shown mercy.
Blessed are the pure in heart, for they will see God. Matthew 5:5–8

We baptized our firstborn, our daughter, in Arizona, where we lived, a thousand miles from either grandparent; so an old retired preacher and his wife told us they would be there and take the traditional grandparents' role, which meant, among other things, Mrs. Verduin said, taking the baby out of church should she get fussy. Rev. and Mrs. Leonard Verduin were Arizona "snowbirds" we came to meet and love, and their participating in our daughter's baptism was something I will never forget.

Rev. Verduin was born and reared in a tiny Dutch-American colony smack dab in the middle of South Dakota's Rosebud Reservation. I'll always remember the stories he told about his childhood out there in all that open land among the Brule Sioux.

But then, there are lots of things I won't forget about Rev. Leonard Verduin, and maybe most basic because most useful to me was his singular insistence that the real, honest-to-God truth is never circular, that is, it never has just one center. Instead, it's always elliptical – it always has two cen-

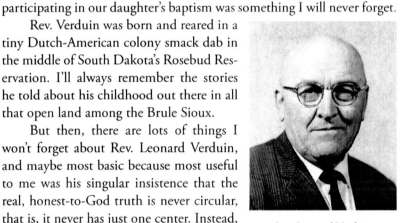

Rev. Leonard Verduin

ters, never one. For instance, Jesus Christ was both God and man. How is that possible? I don't know – it just is, or he isn't who he said he was. Or this: freedom of speech means I can write anything I want; well, not just *anything*. If I sling slimy river mud at someone, a downright lie, then what I said is a bloody, muddy sin, if not a crime. There is no such thing as total freedom of speech because even freedom has limits. Thus, my old friend would say, truth always has two centers.

I thought of Verduin this morning when reading Mother Teresa, who confesses her own exhaustion on the streets of Calcutta. "It does not go so easily when a person has to be on one's feet from morning until evening," she tells her mentor and friend in a letter. "But still, everything is for Jesus," she writes; "so like that everything is beautiful, even though it is difficult" (25).

Two centers, a paradox, "An apparently absurd or self-contradictory statement or proposition, or a strongly counter-intuitive one, which investigation, analysis, or explanation may nevertheless prove to be well-founded or true." What's beautiful, really, is what isn't.

You know, I don't think I was raised to think it might be. When I was a kid, we used to sing, "I'd rather have Jesus than silver and gold" and a host of other lyrics that promised joy from suffering or divine beauty in tribulation. How about this: blessed are the poor in spirit.

Why on earth do I think her statement is paradoxical? Maybe because a gadzillion ads – on print and screen and wherever else – always promise something else. Ad men and women have changed me to believe in skin cream, in Caribbean cruises, and in the ecstasy of twin bathtubs.

How can anything be both difficult and beautiful?

That I see her claim as a paradox this morning is maybe a mark of how far I've strayed from the truth I learned as a child.

Really, what Mother Teresa says is nothing more than biblical truth. I'm the one full of mud. Shine on me, Lord. Shine on me.

PRAYER: What's not difficult to understand, Lord, is that the values of Christ run somehow contrary to the values of the world in which we live. What is difficult is living by values that make it clear to us what isn't beautiful really, by grace, is. Help us to aspire to Christ's unconditional love, to work at being your own hands in this, your world. Amen.

XVII. A Crucifix

He said to them, "How foolish you are, and how slow to believe all that the prophets have spoken! Did not the Messiah have to suffer these things and then enter his glory?" Luke 24:25–26

I have, above my desk, a crucifix my sister gave me. She'd become frustrated because she really didn't know what to do with it. She knew it wasn't "ours" exactly, meaning roughly, "Protestant," but she understood at the same time that the cross adorned with the suffering Christ – a hefty crucifix, by the way – was nothing to sneeze at. A proud old Roman Catholic client she visited regularly in her job as a social worker bestowed it upon her as a loving gift. But that crucifix made her feel uncomfortable, as if she couldn't – or shouldn't – somehow own it.

I know what she meant; that big thing seems, well, too bloody gothic for a real evangelical. We like our crosses clean and shiny, not adorned with the semi-clad body of a suffering Jesus. Somebody put up three crosses in a new subdivision here, right along the street. Nice. Comfortably pious. They're all empty. I can't imagine the same person would put them up adorned with bodies – that would be unsettling, even, well, unpleasant.

We're all about "resurrection," after all. Evangelicals want to tell the story of holy week by way of its grand finale, a rolled-away stone and burial garments folded neatly as if the grave were actually a five-star hotel.

Traditionally, at least, that perspective is not as true of Roman Catholics – and certainly not Mother Teresa, who led her life as someone who believed deeply that "sharing Christ" had less to do with putting a fish on her bumper, a cross on her lawn, or a tract in a toilet stall than placing herself as close as she could to his suffering self every last day of her life. Honestly, that idea is as foreign to an evangelical mind like mine as Jesus Christ being a Dakota warrior, clothed in feathers and beads.

Mother Teresa thought of herself, remember, as "his bride," and her longing to be with him actually began on the cross, in his passion. She wanted to suffer with him, to hurt, to thirst. She wanted nails through her hands, if not literally, metaphorically. She wanted to be up there on that cross, sharing the pain of his broken body. She looked forward to pain. She relished it. She made his misery her joy. The crosses in her lives weren't clean, weren't bright, weren't shiny; they were a feature of an attractively thought out landscape design.

Mother Teresa "longed for complete union with Christ," her spiritual biographer says; and because she did, she "could not do otherwise than be united to Him in His suffering" (25).

My sister couldn't just toss that big crucifix, and her brother can't either. It stays right up here on my wall. It seems

to me that the image of the suffering Christ is something I missed, growing up Calvinist, growing up Evangelical. It may well not have been part of my world, but it can't be edited out of the story, not even for pious reasons.

PRAYER: Maybe we'd rather not think about the suffering you endured for our sin. Maybe we'd rather simply think of the eternal joy of the resurrection than the bloody sacrifice you gave, for us, on the cross and in the grave. Bless us, Lord, with a measure of your own endurance to sanctify us, to strengthen us for the journey you've assigned to each of us. Amen.

XVIII. Ambassador of Joy

"Shout aloud and sing for joy, people of Zion, for great is the Holy One of Israel among you." Isaiah 12:6

There's something so elemental about Mother Teresa's success that when you witness it, you're shocked at its simplicity. "Every Sunday I visit the poor in Calcutta's slums," she wrote in letter. "I cannot help them, because I do not have anything, but I go to give them joy" (27).

Ambassador of Joy. It's that simple.

Because she had nothing in her pockets, she didn't have to refuse beggars. Quite simply, she had nothing to give them except joy, which is, of course, a marvelous gift – and very, very expensive.

Great cheerleaders don't win ball games, and everyone knows you can't reverse malnutrition with a smile, fight disease with sheer happiness, nor deliver people from hapless poverty by a winning personality.

Some significant criticism of Mother Teresa and her work begins with that knowledge, the assessment that just being nice isn't enough. That criticism is understandable. But it can't deny her gift.

What Mother Teresa brought to the poorest of the poor, and gave away freely, was essential for life: she brought them joy – *joy* as a synonym for *love*. In the same letter, she tells the story of a mother whose family suffered immensely, a woman who "did not utter even a word of complaint about her poverty," a woman who begged Mother Teresa to return: "Oh, Ma, come again! Your smile brought sun into this house" (27).

Mother Teresa brought that family the sun.

I don't have neighbors so deeply impoverished. I don't know anyone who doesn't know from whence his or her next meal will come. Those sad children with extended bellies – you've seen them in a ton of photographs – live somewhere in a world other than my own. I'm a long ways from Sudan and all the way around the world from Calcutta.

But then, I suppose, want has a thousand faces. And I can, just as nimbly as she did, lug in the sun, even as she did. Or *could*, if I wanted.

PRAYER: Lord, make me an instrument of your peace, an ambassador of joy. Amen.

XIX. HER COMPACT

"Be still and know that I am God. . . ." Psalm 46:10

Some years go, in a chapel speech at Liberty University, the largest evangelical college in the world, former Governor Rick Perry, then a candidate for President of the United States, talked openly about the nature of his faith in a testimonial that rather notably lacked the fire and brimstone he's known for when he speaks about politics. By all reports, he was reserved and very personal when he spoke of being someone who didn't so much turn to God as he *was* turned.

> My faith journey is not the story of someone who turned to God because I wanted to. It was because I had nowhere else to turn. I was 27. I'd been an officer in the United States Air Force commanding a fairly substantial piece of sophisticated equipment, telling men and women what to do. But I was lost spiritually and emotionally. And I didn't know how to fix it.[1]

There's much to admire in his humility. I don't share many of his political views, but his speech was, or so say a hundred reports, a performance that was as moving as it was sincere.

Sad, though, that anyone has to talk about it as a "performance." I pity political candidates because, these days, they're damned if they do and damned if they don't talk about faith. Not addressing your relationship to God means staying in the starting blocks forever – or not even getting out of the locker room and into the race.

It's ever so easy to listen to someone like Governor Perry – or President Barack Obama – and distrust what you're hearing. They are politicians, for goodness sake – they'll all say what they need to. For Presidential candidates especially, doing a testimony is almost as important as being capable of taking on the economy. And you're judged. Is all that yapping just so much b.s.? That person's faith ain't nothin' more than politics. Listen.

Father Brian Kolodiejchuk, editor of *Come Be My Light*, says that in April of 1942, Mother Teresa made a significant vow before God. This is how she described it: "I made a vow to God – binding under [pain

---

1 *Huffington Post*, September 14, 2011.

of] mortal sin – to give God anything He may ask, 'Not to refuse him anything'" (34–35).

That vow was, Kolodiejchuk says, one of her "greatest secrets." Only two people on the planet knew what she'd done – she and her confessor; and when, 17 years later, she finally went public with that vow, she admitted, "This is what hides everything in me" (29).

It seems to me, as our preacher said not long ago, that the joy known to those who know the Lord may, paradoxically, be, for us, one of the most difficult things to talk about because the language of faith is so easily manipulated. I don't doubt for a moment Rick Perry has great faith, but he becomes, in a way, a victim of his own politics, as does every aspirant politician, the moment he or she talks about faith, simply because that person is a politician running for office.

It is not particularly easy to talk about faith because, in fact, it is so marvelously easy.

One of the most easily forgotten mandates Christ put on the table was the warning to pray in private, to go where no one can see you. Sometimes, with faith, Jesus might have said, silence is golden.

I wonder whether part of the marvelous spiritual legacy Mother Teresa leaves behind grows from the fact that her own life-changing pledge, the vow she says changed everything in her life – a vow not to refuse God whatever he would ask – was more binding because it *wasn't* broadcast over CNN or written up in a Calcutta mission newsletter. Her witness to his glory in that pledge, that vow, was between the two of them and the two of them only – between her and God.

It's impossible for politicians not to talk about their faith. They must. And because they are who they are – *politicians!* – it's easy to roll your eyes. At any of them.

What Mother Teresa teaches me with this silent vow of hers is the lesson the scriptures offer, the lesson of Psalm 46: "Be still and know that I am God."

PRAYER: Teach us to be circumspect, Lord, teach us a vital and effective rhetoric of faith. Teach us to know when to speak and how to speak about your love. Make our word good because it's yours. Amen.

XX. Possession

"Hear my prayer, LORD, listen to my cry for help; do not be deaf to my weeping. I dwell with you as a foreigner, a stranger, as all my ancestors were." Psalm 39:12

There is, within me, more than a smidgen of my grandfather's DNA, more than a pint or two of his dark Calvinist blood. I think of him often really, a man so driven by the depth of his own sinfulness (he was really a good man) that he would take a kind of perverse pleasure in recounting the darkness of his soul – as in, "if I had one thing to do with my salvation, I'd burn in hell." That kind of thing. Complete with tears. Lots.

He likely had a family background in the old Dutch conventicle tradition, those hotbed small groups where intense devotions ran so emotion-laden that their house meetings became, in no small measure, the church. Some people believe that house churches are the wave of the future. Good night, they have a history, a past – deep meditations for intense sinners whose long prayers in an intimate circle stretched on end-lessly. Grandpa had a heavy dose of that.

Back then, in the early years of the 20th century, I don't think he was unusual. In most churches there were more Harry Dirkses per capita, I'm sure, than there are today. That kind of exhausting, abject confession promised and likely delivered abundant blessings. After all, the finest means by which to glory in the marvelous grace of God almighty was to lie prostrate on the floor in abject selflessness. Grace, for even lowly me!

By all reports, that was my grandpa. It's easy to parody.

But I'm saying that sometime he's in me, too. Maybe more than sometime. Maybe far more than I care to admit.

My mother, his daughter, always wished to be Pentecostal, to speak in tongues, to be ever closer to the Lord than she was, no matter that her son thinks she's dang well close enough. Her son thought such un-quenchable longing is almost a disease. For someone who talked constantly about the love of God, it sometimes seemed to me that she was never an arm's length away, maybe even farther.

She wanted "Blessed Assurance" sung at her husband's funeral be-cause she knew he never shared her tremulous faith. My father never thought much about his salvation, even though he was, as most who know him would say, something of a saint. She's never quite understood his confidence because she was never herself so blessedly assured. If she were, the drama would be over; and I think she liked the drama.

Her son can giggle about all this, but what I'm confessing this morning is that, like it or not, I'm still my mother's son – and my grandpa's grandson. And I feel it most when I read something like this from Mother Teresa: "Why must we give ourselves fully to God? Because God has given Himself to us" (29).

Just blows me away. That logic is so airtight that its undeniable truth makes mincemeat of my feeble attempts at being faithful. She is so absolutely right. Just to be sure, let me say that there are no tears here – I'm not my grandfather's clone. But the way Mother Teresa says what she does here casts a long, sickening shadow over my sinfulness. I admit it.

See, there he is – Grandpa Dirkse. In the flesh.

"I live for God and give up my own self, and in this way induce God to live for me," she wrote. "Therefore to possess God we must allow Him to possess our soul" (29).

Wow. Let me tell you, on that one I'm stricken.

PRAYER: Lord, her logic is airtight here, help us to live by it, sinners as we are. Why must we give ourselves fully to you? Because you gave yourself fully for us. It's that simple and that clear. Give us the courage to live that way, so our deeds are as striking as our words. Amen.

XXI. Getting Along

Oh, that my ways were steadfast in obeying your decrees!
Then I would not be put to shame when I consider all your com-
	mands.
I will praise you with an upright heart as I learn your righteous laws.
I will obey your decrees; do not utterly forsake me.
How can a young person stay on the path of purity?
By living according to your word.
I seek you with all my heart; do not let me stray from your commands.

Psalm 119:5–10

According to the editor of her letters and diaries, Fr. Brian Kolodiejchuk, Mother Teresa believed that in obeying her superiors in the Sisters
of Loreto, she was, in fact, obeying Jesus; in "submitting to their commands, she was submitting to Christ Himself" (31) is the way he puts it.

I confess. That's a way of life I can't imagine.

There's something undeniably saint-like about her inviolable commitment, but something slavish too. If the simple obedience – can I say
"blind obedience"? – to one's superiors is the portal to sainthood, then
I'm a long way from coming through that door.

I can't imagine it was easy to believe that one's superiors spoke for
the Lord – then again, maybe it was easy to believe, just hard to live.
That's not an altogether human problem either.

But somehow it makes sense that Mother Teresa would believe what
she did. If you're going want to be the bride of Christ, if you're going to
commit, via something as permanent as an oath, to live for him always,
every second of the day – no time off, no Expedia getaways – then it
seems to me that some kind of infrastructure to that commitment is, in
fact, essential. In her case, her scaffolding was created by the church – or
The Church.

I mean, no human being ever believed that he or she was one with
Jesus, 24/7, you think? Even David the King often found himself abandoned – see Psalm 13, the "howling" psalm. I hate to be skeptical, but
my guess is no one on the face of the earth ever claimed to have God's
voice in his heart and soul *all the time*. No earthling stays permanently in

some higher world.

It just doesn't happen. In his "Personal Narrative," Jonathan Edwards, the great revivalist Calvinist, claims he suffered long, anguished moments of silence. Emerson tried to lift anyone who'd hear him into bright and shiny moments of revelation, but he certainly didn't stay there himself (read "Experience" sometime). Even Edgar Allen Poe wanted his bizarre verse to lift us, at least for a moment, from our rotten, stinking world. But only for a moment.

Abraham Kuyper's most famous devotional work, *To Be Near Unto God*, is all about helping his loyal followers find their way, at least, to glimpses of glory. Glimpses.

No one I know would say that Christ's voice is *always* within them. But then, I'm not Pentecostal. Maybe if I were. . . .

It's understandable that someone like Mother Teresa, someone as committed to God's near physical presence in her life, would determine that the way to get there, even (and maybe especially) through the silences, is by believing that the words of the boss – her Mother Superior or her bishop, or whoever was in charge in her life – were always the words of the Master.

I've failed badly on that one. But that's a story for another time.

Here's what I'm thinking. We're wired with desire, all of us, for god. That *g* has to be lower case, as in Poe's case; but human beings share an undeniable spiritual aspiration. Mother Teresa, who is without a doubt a saint, attempted to stifle the doubts she had (and they were considerable) by believing that whatever church authorities said was the gospel. When her superiors spoke, the voice belonged to God (upper case). What was required from her, in response, was, of course, total obedience.

I've never been so sure. But there's no doubt in my mind – and soul – that I too want God. As hard as it is for an old Calvinist like me to admit it, I think we all do, even if our aspiration doesn't make us saints.

Maybe what makes all of us want to get there is that we can't.

Only by his doing. Only by grace.

I'm sure she believed that too.

PRAYER: Some marvelously blessed souls get along royally with those who are their superiors, Lord. Some people are blessed with bosses, parents, supervisors, teachers, administrators who lead like servants. Bless us with grace, with circumspection, with respect, with selflessness, Lord, even when swallowing what's going on gets really tough. Make us instruments of your peace. Amen.

XXII. In the Silence of the Heart

> When he opened the seventh seal, there was silence in heaven for about half an hour. Revelation 8:1

Walking home from school for me has always meant walking west into what is, this daylight-shortened time of year, the first warm glow of sunset. For years I've told myself – especially during frenetic seasons like this one, exam time – that someday I'm just going to keep walking into all that buttery glory, going to head west like Huck Finn and millions of others who hear the siren song of a dreamy new life. Someday, instead of stopping, I'll just keep walking. Like an old bull bison, I'll leave the herd forever, wander out somewhere into the hills along the river, and hunker down.

Sounds good right now. Well, maybe a little cold. Ah, big deal – I've got a down jacket.

I've got eleventy-seven papers to read, more pouring in daily. Today, I'm off to speak at a high school chapel, I've got two big speeches to write, an exam to give (36 more papers) this afternoon, and a junk drawer full of little complexities too mean to mention. But then I'm but a semester away from being able to just keep walking. Just a semester.

I'm sure I'm not as busy as Mother Teresa. I'm sure that those Calcutta streets full of poor folks made demands on her and her time that may well have prompted her to look up wistfully toward beaming sunsets too. The dogged vow she took – the promise of utter loyalty to the Lord's will – created a listening ear in her that probably never shut down because she wanted, above all else, to hear the voice of God obediently, never to miss even his most indistinct whispers.

Which is why, I suppose, she loved to tell herself and others that "in the silence of the heart God speaks" (32).

The idea strikes me as medieval because I really ought to be connected – always. I ought to have all the gizmos. Last week our grandson stayed around after dinner and begged to watch Ninja Pandas or some such thing. Begged. I know why, because it was difficult for him – as it is for any of us who are tuned in 24/7 – to entertain silence. He has to be connected. Me too. My smartphone keeps silence at bay, even though it doesn't speak unless spoken too. I read the *Huffington Post* far more than the gospels, *Drudge* more than King David. I'm serious.

I know Mother Teresa is right, and so does anyone else who listens. "In the silence of the heart, God speaks." Maybe that's why I'm addicted to getting up early every morning.

But then maybe not. I know well and good that every little whisper in my ear isn't the voice of God.

Still, we all know she's right: Listen again: "In the silence of the heart God speaks."

Some of my ethnic and religious ancestors stuck a copy of Abraham Kuyper's *To Be Near Unto God* into the pockets of their barn jackets a century ago or more, so special were those meditations to them. The focus of Kuyper's meds is achieving moments of eternal bliss, just moments. "To be near unto God," for Abraham Kuyper, meant maintaining a daily walk within whispering distance of God's own voice. No residents of this world can possibly live near unto God 24/7, Kuyper might have said, but we can come blessedly close for occasional divine moments.

I don't doubt that Prime Minister Kuyper would have heartily assented to Mother Teresa: "In the silence of the heart God speaks."

It's just before six. I've said enough.

PRAYER: Lord Almighty, help us feel comfortable in the silences, grant us purpose and devotion as a means of securing it. Once there, speak to us, to our hearts. Make us more and more your own. Amen.

XXIII. CHEERFULNESS

Therefore, my dear friends, as you have always obeyed – not only in my presence, but now much more in my absence – continue to work out your salvation with fear and trembling. . . . Philippians 2:12

I don't buy it totally. It strikes me as half-truth, which is, at times, even more deceptive than a lie. I understand what she says, I even have some sympathies with the idea, but finally I think she was wrong. Well, half wrong. "Cheerfulness is a sign of a generous and mortified person who, forgetting all things, even herself, tries to please her God in all she does for souls" (33).

A *mortified* person is someone whose old man (or woman) of sin is dead as doornail. It has nothing to do with being absolutely *mortified* by what stupidity came out of your cousin Ezra's mouth last Sunday. When your sin is, so to speak, behind you, she's saying, cheerfulness becomes a habit. That's sweet. I'm listening but not convinced.

"Cheerfulness is often a cloak which hides a life of sacrifice, continual union with God, fervor and generosity" (33). I don't know that I believe that totally either, but I like it. Run into an ever-cheerful person, she says, and you'll be with someone whose deep devotion to God is a constant.

I'm still listening, but she's starting to sound as tinny as a cheerleader – "don't worry, be happy." "A person who has this gift of cheerfulness very often reaches a great height of perfection" (33).

Warning lights are going off. Even the apostle Paul would draw an eyebrow here, so I am not alone, nor am I too much a Calvinist to scale that perfection mountain. In my book, the perfect is sometimes the enemy of the good.

But I'm still listening. After all, this is Mother Teresa. "For God loves a cheerful giver and He takes close to His heart the religious He loves" (33).

She's far more sure about such things than I am, but okay. But then how do you reconcile that idea with the treasures that darkness and sheer doubt have given us? Much of our music arises from thwarted human aspiration, from the dead opposite of Disney-level cheerfulness. America's finest gift to the arts is the blues, doleful music drawn from the sad lives of African-American folk musicians. The blues are beautiful, even inspiring. But Lord knows they're not cheerful. And neither are some psalms, come to think of it.

And then this: "When I see someone sad, I always think, she is refusing something to Jesus" (33). I've known too much depression to buy that one. It's something you might whisper in your own ear, but telling someone else that his or her sorrow comes from lack of faith can be deadly when persistent darkness isn't just inflamed moodiness. Believe me. "Your problem, kid, is you're just not right with God." While that idea may not be all wrong, as therapy it can kill.

Mississippi John Hurt

Mother Teresa may well have believed what she says about cheerfulness. She may have used that sentiment to scold herself – that's understandable. But if her own confessions are true, if her diaries and letters reveal someone who fought off the darkness – and they do! – then she couldn't really have believed it herself. She wasn't always cheerful because she wasn't always something beautiful for Jesus. Even Mother Teresa wasn't perfect, wasn't always cheerful. And she knew it. And she tells us as much.

"Therefore, my dear friends," says the letter to the Philippians, "as you have always obeyed – not only in my presence, but now much more in my absence – continue to work out your salvation with fear and trembling." "With fear and trembling." Those words are not necessarily cheerful.

She's not the gospel on cheerfulness, but she's not totally wrong either. It's good to know I'm not alone.

PRAYER: Help us up, Lord, when we're down. Put a smile on our faces, help us light up the lives of others. Forgive us when we don't shine. Lend us your light, your eternal light. Amen.

XXIV. THE LITTLE STUFF

Then I heard every creature in heaven and on earth and under the earth and on the sea, and all that is in them, saying: "To him who sits on the throne and to the Lamb be praise and honor and glory and power, for ever and ever!" Revelation 5:13

To the good God nothing is little. . . . (34)

You know? – I really ought to print that line on a t-shirt: "To the good God nothing is little." It's hers – Mother Teresa's – and it's just plain beautiful.

But then, maybe I think so just because I'm getting old.

How is it that retired people get such a kick out of gardening? Why, for pity sake, does the appearance of that gorgeous cardinal or her lovely husband just outside our window just light up our day? Last night, my wife and I had a quiet supper together alone for the first time in a week, and it felt something like what I little I know of heaven. What's that about anyway?

The world simply shrinks the older you get. That's what I'm thinking.

Yesterday, I got a card from a man I don't know. He says he's been reading a book of my meditations over and over again, and they're good, words I ground up down here in this basement. It was that kind of letter. Just a card. That's it. Just a little homemade card. Made my day. Shoot, made my week. Little things.

A kid says something on his way out the classroom. Maybe it was an okay class that day, and as he's walking out, he says, "Have a good afternoon, Professor." I feel like I'm somebody. Little things.

A sunset. A windless, warm February afternoon. The faint whisper of spring. A raucous orchestra of birds in the morning sun once again, or the long glowing promise of an orange dawn.

Bad knees, leaky plumbing, sore feet, a testy stomach – there's no end to the tribulations of aging. And yet, sometimes it just seems that I find myself, these days, a joyful victim of a transformed aesthetic. Instead of looking past life's seeming givens, its otherwise incidentals, you take joy in 'em. A plain old bowl of cereal starts to taste like a feast, I swear it.

Maybe that's what theologians mean by sanctification. Maybe the death of the old, young man begets the quickening of the new, old one. Count the paradox in that line. Okay, maybe it's silly, but, dang it! – it's cute.

Mother Teresa used to tell her sisters that to God everything is small, and therefore everything is beautiful because everything is divine. Isn't that wonderful? "Because he makes them," she'd say, "they are very great. He cannot make anything small; they are infinite" (34).

Rain on parched soil. Newbie buds on the maples out front. An old hymn you thought you'd forgotten.

At the funeral of a man I never knew, one little photograph of he and his wife just after the war, totally in love – I remember that darling snapshot, so full of life, far better than the shape of his face as he lay in the open coffin. I still see it. I wish I could show you.

Or how about this? Just beside me now, the last three segments of an orange I've been eating slowly ever since I sat down at this computer. I pull 'em apart, one at a time because of the juicy blessing I get with each little tart explosion of lovely taste.

Now there are two.

"Be faithful in little practices of love, of little sacrifices," Mother Teresa used to say (34). Such things make you Christ-like.

Could it be possible that aging makes that easier?

Don't ask me tomorrow. This may just be a good morning.

Besides, the orange is gone.

But then maybe that cardinal will show up. I should be so blessed.

PRAYER: For your world, Lord, we thank you – for the little things that come visible when we see the world with the eyes of experience. For experience itself, Lord, we thank you. For sanctifying us, as we sing along through life, we are grateful. Amen.

XXV. Knowing God's Will

Do not conform to the pattern of this world, but be transformed by the renewing of your mind. Then you will be able to test and approve what God's will is – his good, pleasing and perfect will. Romans 12:2

Probably the most famous line in all of theater belongs to Prince Hamlet: "To be or not to be." Won't be long and I'll be going through *Hamlet* again, and it'll be my job, to try to explain why that ubiquitous question of his is somehow timeless, even though few of us struggle with suicide or revenge for a murdered father.

Really difficult decisions about what to do are made more trying, or so it seems, by a transcendent, even eternal dimension to our decision-making, something we call "God's will." Joel Nederhood, in his book of devotions, *The Forever People*, claims that what Jesus himself gives us in the single petition of the Lord's Prayer is the wish that we human beings would become more like the angels, simply taking God's orders without question. "The reference to heaven in the perfect prayer," he says ("Your will be done on earth as it is in heaven"), "reminds us that there is a realm where the will of God is absolutely supreme." Therefore, he says, "Those who want to live eternal life beginning now realize that God's will must be supreme," a realization and commitment that should make Hamlet's indecision silly, if not, dare I say it? – sinful.

Emphasis on *should*. If only complete submission to the will of God were that simple. In my life at least, determining God's will has never been a piece of cake. Am I alone here?

Mother Teresa, on the other hand, had no such problem. When, occasionally, she was accused of acting without thinking, she excused herself on the basis of her commitment, her vow, to do God's will always. *Always.*

She had to have been blessed with a mind cleansed of filtering agents, nor could she have a dime's worth of cynicism. She never heard that still small voice that says, so frequently (at least to me and Hamlet), "well, hold on just a minute here."

I once wrote an article about a retired missionary who lit up my day with jubilant recitations of the abundantly good life on the mission field.

I came away from that interview truly blessed. The woman breathed joy.

Sometime later, another old missionary told me that the woman who'd blessed me with her stories had been indefatigable on the mission field, but her overflowing energy sometimes got her into trouble. If she was scheduled for a meeting, she'd forget in a heartbeat if, on the way, she spotted some children playing under a tree. She felt compelled to tell them about Jesus. Meetings be hanged.

She knew God's will.

I couldn't help think of her when I read that Mother Teresa "developed the habit of responding immediately to the demands of the present moment," something she did so regularly that "this swiftness to act was misinterpreted and taken for impetuousness or lack of prudence" (34). Maybe that caliber of commitment is packaged with any call to mission work – you simply and wholeheartedly equate your mission with God's will. End of subject.

As for me and my house, we're more Hamlet-like, forever between a rock and hard place. I probably think too much; and, right now, smarting under Nederhood's admonition, I'll probably not repeat that petition from the Lord's prayer again without seeing my own ink-faced sin in the mirror – "thy will be done." Sounds so stinkin' easy. Just like that – no brooding, no worrying, no sleepless nights. Just do it.

One of the few theological words with earthy Anglo-Saxon roots is *atonement*, which means, as it says, to be "at one" with God. I know two now-deceased women, missionaries both, who obviously got closer than I am to being at one with God.

But my cynical mind says so did David Koresh and Harold Camping and a thousand other cultists who thought they were "at one," but were not.

There I go questioning again. I'm hopeless.

May God have mercy on me. And Hamlet.

PRAYER: Give us wisdom and sound hearing, Lord, to help us know your will in our lives. No matter how old or young, open our hearts to your word in every manner and language you use to speak to us. And always keep us close. In your son's name, Amen.

XXVI. Lugging the Mace

Whatever you do, work at it with all your heart, as working for the
Lord, not for human masters. . . . Colossians 3:23

Sometime in the 16th century it might have been appropriate for an
academic like myself to carry an ungainly tool with no apparent use, up
a long hallway, leading a procession of hundreds of black-robes; but I'm
not at all sure about today. Seems silly but I'm doing it, one last time on
Friday.

The ungainly tool is called a mace, and while this one is beautifully created from ceramics and oak, this thing – it's huge really – is
fundamentally anachronistic because whatever vital function a mace actually performed some millennia ago, that function is long gone. So some
stooge – me this year – carries this four-foot club up on the stage and tells
the graduates exactly where to sit, performing some medieval role no one
understands, not even the mace-lugger.

On Friday I will carry this thing like a majorette leading a black
phalanx of enrobed weirdoes in mortar boards and dancing tassels. I'm
not making this up. Thousands of people will be there to see it happen,
and the whole place will wonder who on earth that clown is, the one carrying that ridiculously big stick? – ye olde court jester?

I had to practice yesterday, walk through the exercise, an exercise my
long-time mace-toting predecessor took as seriously as Moses did when
he raised his staff above the Red Sea. Me? – I just roll my eyes. "It's a
privilege," the President told me when he conned me into it. Okay, then
why doesn't he do it?

Yesterday I sat in a pew before 350 students who filled the stage and
got instructions on how not to let their tassels get in the way when the
school-appointed photographer snaps their pictures when they get their
sheepskin. Mostly, those soon-to-be grads looked dumbfounded.

High school graduations are really quite silly since basically you get
a diploma for showing up. Oh, here and there one might encounter a test
or a paper, but the national lament about our country's stinking educa-
tional system begins with high schools. Internationally, our third-graders
are doing fine. Somewhere at the end of middle school things fall apart.

But college graduations mean something; if nothing else, the adding machine stops going ca-ching. Once again, this Friday, the mere fact that kids are finally graduating from college creates such a huge collective parental sigh that oxygen levels in the chapel get dangerously low.

But yesterday there I sat. Honestly, the whole bunch of 'em – the seniors – looked, well, scared. Who can blame them? Tons of them carry loans worth thousands of dollars, most of them are embarking on a life none of them foresee clearly. Saturday morning they'll wake up in an economy that sports eight percent unemployment. Wherever they start their first job, they'll begin at the bottom.

Grad speeches rarely sink in because beneath those mortar boards nobody is thinking much about wisdom. Seniors are little better than mannequins. I don't have a clue who spoke at any of my graduations. I've given those speeches and been no more memorable, I'm sure.

But this morning I just read a line in Mother Teresa that makes all sorts of sense, something I wish I could impart to all those enrobed students I'll be leading into the chapel on Friday. Maybe we ought to put it on t-shirts and make every one of them wear it beneath their robes. Here's what MT said: "Don't look for big things, just do small things with great love" (34). Isn't that a wonderful line?

Maybe I ought to print it on a flag and sail it from the mace.

And then this: "The smaller the thing, the greater must be our love" (34). That's all that needs be said, methinks. If we'd all listen to Mother Teresa, we'd live in a different world. Even me. Blush.

And that stupid mace – "small things with great love." Okay. I swear I won't roll my eyes.

PRAYER: Our days and nights are heavy-laden sometimes with deeds we'd rather not do, as a matter of fact. Give us some a measure of your grace big enough to do the small things with great love. You, Lord, who love us, even in our brazen haughtiness. In your Son's blessed name, Amen.

XXVII. "I THIRST"

"I am thirsty." John 19:28

Sometimes people here in the upper Midwest claim we're blessed with only two seasons: winter and Fourth of July. The line works, I think, for two reasons: one, winters can be brutal; and two, so can Fourth of July.

When we moved to Iowa from Arizona, we didn't expect to be clobbered by heat, but we were. The house we rented was not air-conditioned, and, that first July, we nearly died – that's overstatement. What we'd left was higher temps, but what we'd discovered was humidity.

Right about now, mid-summer, nothing dispatches thirst like lemonade. Pink, white, raspberry – no matter. It's a reminder of a boyhood bucking bales when icy canning jars full of the stuff were the only antidote to heat stroke. That's overstatement too.

We just finished a sojourn in New Mexico, where we hiked over murky lava flows and through elegant sandstone at elevations that sucked your body dry. *Always pack water. Drink it.* Parks and trails at 7000 feet don't pussyfoot; their signs use the command form. Water is life. I drank buckets.

I've spent most of my adult life believing that if we underplay anything at all about Jesus Christ it's his human side. The great mystery of his existence is that he was, at once, both God and man. Impossible, yet there he is, both. Where we underestimate him, I've often thought, is in his humanity. We like him as Lord and Savior, but he could be almost unfeeling at times – witness his seeming disregard for his own mother when he started out on his own in the temple. If you want to follow me, he told his disciples, forget Mom and Dad – actions he modeled himself.

He was human. Jesus Christ was human, too, not just Lord and Maker and King and Redeemer. He pulled human flesh as if it were spandex, for Pete's sake – and mine.

Therefore, "I am thirsty" is an utterance I've often considered to be a clear indication of his humanity. The physical agony of the cross, far beyond my imagination, prompted very human needs – he got thirsty, horrifically so. He was human. Be careful, I might have said – and still would – about over-spiritualizing him.

Then there's Mother Teresa, whose very ministry was created – by her own account – by her acceptance of that very Good Friday utterance – "I thirst" (41).

> Why does Jesus say "I thirst"? What does it mean? Something so hard to explain in words – . . . "I thirst" is something much deeper than just Jesus saying "I love you." Until you know, deep inside that Jesus thirsts for you – you can't begin to know who He wants to be for you. Or who He wants you to be for Him. (42)

That's what MT believed.

Jesus Christ was Mother Teresa's sole motivational speaker, and his words, especially those uttered in his agony, were her rallying cry. She transformed his thirst into a metaphor and spent her life working to quench the emptiness he felt at Calvary, an emptiness satisfied only by the poor – their love and their souls. His thirst for them became her soul's motivation.

She saw Jesus dehydrated, wearied, nearly dead; and she sought to bring him relief on the streets of Calcutta by satisfying his thirst for those poor he loved so greatly.

It may well be I've been wrong for all these years. Perhaps in stressing his humanity, I've neglected his divinity. Perhaps in taking him literally, I've not seen him spiritually up there on the cross at Golgotha, body and soul dehydrated, his heart overworking to pump his dehydrated blood because he wants, more than anything, not just water but, as MT might say it, those he loves, his people, splashing over him, gushing with love.

That's the way she read it, and that's the way she lived in Calcutta. Something to consider, even in our muggiest July.

PRAYER: Thank you for her deeds, Lord, this saint, Mother Teresa. Thank you for what she did to those who suffer life's most significant deprivations. But thank you too for her words, for her thoughts, for her almost instinctive righteousness. Thank you for showing her – and us – the meaning of your own words, your own thirst. Amen.

XXVIII. Bringing Him and Meeting Him

"The King will reply, 'Truly I tell you, whatever you did for one of the least of these brothers and sisters of mine, you did for me.'" Matthew 25:40

In *Chant of the Night*, Cornelius Kuipers' 1930s novel about mission work in the Zuni pueblo of New Mexico, a young Zuni named Ametolan agrees to take three Anglo missionaries for a day-long hike up Zuni Mountain, a deeply sacred place to his people. As they climb, they learn some things about the Zunis' history of great suffering, first at the hands of the Spanish, then at the hands of missionaries from the south, from Mexico, stories illustrated by hand and footholds carved into the sheer sides of the mountain so the people could escape death.

The white folks love the stories, but they joke around; they don't revere the place, as does Ametolan. When one of the Anglos says she'd like to meet the god of the Zuni mountain because "he must be some guy," "the party laughed," says Kuipers, "but not Ametolan."

Kuipers was himself an Anglo missionary who spent decades in the Zuni pueblo. That he would criticize his colleagues and fellow Christians' nonchalance is interesting and, in its own way, lovely. He breaks the stereotype of Christian missionaries who were often what Native people determined them to be – piously disguised scouts for a cultural cavalry who sought, as did the U.S. Army, the demise of all American indigenous people.

Zuni Mission, Zuni Pueblo, NM, circa 1935

I don't claim to know anything about missiology. I've never been a missionary, and I don't know how missionaries are trained. But I do know something about how Christian mission has often blundered with Native people, killing them and their spirit with their own Godly intentions. Almost a century ago, a missionary named Cornelius Kuipers seemed to understand that too – and he used his novels to try to explain what he'd discovered on the mission field, not to the Zunis, who needed no explanation, but to his own people, Anglo Christians.

How did he come to understand that banter in holy places, even pagan holy places, is always off-key? The title of his only nonfiction book is *Zuni Also Prays,* which is to say, don't demean people. Pride is the first of seven deadlies, spiritual pride the most hideous. Just remember, Zuni also prays.

This morning Mother Teresa taught me something that Cornelius Kuipers would have liked. Mother Teresa took to heart that absolutely central passage of the gospel recorded in Matthew 25: "Whatever you did for one of the least of these brothers and sisters of mine, you did for me." While she dedicated her entire life to bringing Christ to the poor on the streets of Calcutta, she was equally sure, strange as this may sound, that when she met the poor, she met Jesus. She not only brought Christ, she met him in the wasted streets. She looked into the faces of the poor and, quite literally, saw Jesus.

When I read the novels of Cornelius Kuipers, novels meant for his people, I can't help thinking that he too saw Jesus there in the Zuni, a vision he knew very well might be difficult to relate to people back home.

Really, all of this isn't just about missiology; it's about the very character of the Christian life, don't you think?

PRAYER: Open our eyes, Lord – open them to the riches of your world, your creation; and help us to see in others, in all others – even those we might not like or even tolerate – that Jesus is there, too, in them, in the image of God each of them hold. Amen.

XXIX. To be a Saint

To the church of God in Corinth, to those sanctified in Christ Jesus
and called to be his holy people, together with all those everywhere
who call on the name of our Lord Jesus Christ – their Lord and ours.
. . . 1 Corinthians 1:2.

Sometimes I envy the Roman Catholic world because they help the
rest of us identify who is and who isn't a saint. Protestants, after all, use
the word *saint* almost like a metaphor – the saint who, out of nowhere,
stops along a highway to help with a flat; the saint in the parking lot who
picks up your wallet and sends it home, leaving every cent of the $100
you'd just withdrawn from an ATM. You know – "Gee, I swear that guy
is a saint."

Not really. But almost.

There's no *almost* in the Roman Catholic tradition – well, there have
been also-rans, I'm sure; but the Vatican finally judges who is and who
isn't, recognizing, even certifying sainthood. Getting into that elite club
is not a cakewalk either.

In September of 1946, Mother Teresa was on a train to an annual
spiritual retreat, when she heard directly from Jesus, who spoke in no
uncertain terms, telling her, not asking her, to get out of the education
business altogether and bring love, in Calcutta, to the poorest of the
poor. "Come be my light," he told her.

In intervals, this conversation continued throughout the entire retreat. Jesus was calling, calling her name, calling her mission. The language was clear and forceful but memorably endearing. She told others
that he spoke to her lovingly calling her: "My own spouse" and "My own
little one" (44).

The mission, however, was daunting. She claimed – and the church
certifiably recognizes – that it was the very voice of Jesus Christ speaking
to her, not once but many times during that retreat: "Come, come, carry
Me into the holes of the poor. Come, be My light" (44).

The book I'm reading, titled *Come Be My Light*, chooses to print
these lines, the lines Jesus spoke, in italics, like this: *"Come, come, carry
Me into the holes of the poor. Come, be My light."* I've walked through doz-

ens of language and grammar texts in my 40 years of teaching English, but I never encountered a punctuation rule that applies to quotes from God. I don't know who chose to put Christ's words into italics, but it makes sense that someone would determine that, on the page before me, his words deserve some kind of unique ornamentation.

The 1946 retreat at Darjeeling, India, determined Mother's Teresa's future. After all, she'd heard from Jesus. She'd listened to his voice. She had no choice but to follow.

I'm not sure how to talk about what the Roman Catholics call "interior locutions" because, the Lord knows, millions of people, over time, have heard voices they registered as emanating from God, many of them demanding bizarre things. I'm not sure how those direct quotes should be printed, but I'm willing to give the Roman Catholic authorities the freedom to believe that, in Mother Teresa's case, the voice was so real and true and divine that we simply have to italicize.

Here's the truth we live with, Roman Catholic and Protestant, all believers: that such communication seems impossible doesn't mean it doesn't happen.

Maybe Mother Teresa did hear him on the train to, and all during, her retreat. Maybe Jesus Christ, from his throne at the right hand of God almighty, decided to stop the train so as to speak his word to a bird-like Albanian schoolteacher in India. The Roman Catholics believe he did because, in part, they know she listened.

To Roman Catholics, Mother Teresa is a saint.

On that most all of us agree, even though our two traditions ascribe varying definitions.

Maybe I'm too much the Protestant, too much the skeptic, but I think I would have avoided the italics.

Still, in my book, she is a saint.

PRAYER: Thank you for saints and saintliness, Lord. Thank you for giving us human beacons in the darkness of our world, shining lights who selflessly give from streams of mercy you allow to flow through their hearts. Make us all saints. Bless us, each of us, with saintliness in your son's name. Amen.

XXX. Voices from on High

When Mary reached the place where Jesus was and saw him, she fell
at his feet and said, "Lord, if you had been here, my brother would
not have died." When Jesus saw her weeping, and the Jews who had
come along with her also weeping, he was deeply moved in spirit and
troubled. John 11:32–33

In the 1820 throes of the Second Great Awakening western New
York was aflame with spiritual passions. All kinds of people were seeing
visions, dreaming dreams, Joseph Smith among them. Smith was living
there at the time, speaking directly to God – his father and grandfather
and dozens of others had too. No big deal.

Joseph Smith

What's more, Smith was a scryer,
someone who could be professionally em-
ployed to see things psychically – "have
crystal ball, will travel." Even better, he
made his living by treasure hunting, seek-
ing buried fortunes in fields. Enough. I'm
prejudicing the case. Mr. Smith told those
who knew him that he was regularly visited by an angel named Morini, who told
him the location of some buried golden
plates Smith couldn't find when he went
to retrieve them. However, sometime later,
he did. Those plates were inscribed in a language Smith called "reformed
Egyptian" and therefore needed translation.

When finally the plates were translated, what they said became *The
Book of the Mormon.*

Today, no one knows where those plates are, nor whether there is or
has ever been a language called "reformed Egyptian."

It was a vision, Joseph Smith said, Joseph the dreamer. And it was
also the beginning of the Church of Jesus Christ of Latter-day Saints.

To me at least, this vision thing is really tough. Mother Teresa was so
sure that Christ himself had spoken to her during the retreat in Darjeeling that she likely had trouble sleeping – if God wants you to do something and you're his little bride, how can he be denied? When she told her

spiritual mentor, he told her to forget about it.

She couldn't. Mother Teresa became the Bible's own persistent widow (Luke 18), constantly pressing everyone including her bishop to speak to Rome about what she'd been simply told to do – to give her permission to go into the darkest corners of Calcutta's ghettos and bring love to those who know so very little.

The bishop waited, not sure, so had her spiritual mentor. Time passed. Mother Teresa was upset; her letters burn with her frustration. The command was vivid. The responsibility was hers. She had to act. The church was in her way.

It took some time for the bishop to allow her to move in the direction she felt called to do, but months later Mother Teresa was given authority to minister to the unloved of Calcutta, a task Jesus himself, she said, had instructed her to take up.

Joseph Smith claimed to hear from on high too, but he determined to start his own fellowship. He didn't wait to hear from church authorities. He didn't have to cool it. He didn't have to bow to any authority but his own.

I fear I will forever be skeptical of those who claim to hear Jesus' own voice. I don't know why exactly, but I am.

The Mormons today are wonderful people. Last election, a Mormon was one of the candidates for the Presidency of the United States; another, with totally opposite politics, was the Senate Majority Leader.

But if I'm going to believe that Jesus Christ chooses individuals with whom to speak, as Smith and Mother Teresa both claimed, I'm going to side with "the little bride of Christ," not because I knew or know either of them, but because one of those visions was tested strenuously by church folks who may well have been as skeptical as I was. They didn't want to believe it either, and who knows but that they granted her wishes over against their own better judgment.

Did Jesus Christ, son of God, speak to Mother Teresa on a train to Darjeeling?

Maybe he did, but what he told her is something she'd heard before – a command to minister to those in need wherever you find them. He'd said it before, after all, in ways all of us have heard.

PRAYER: You speak to us in so many ways, Lord. We hear your voice in the thunder, in the clear blue sky, in an afternoon in a lawn chair. Give us ears to listen, to hear what you say up above the noise of our everyday lives. Sharpen our hearing, Lord – and open our eyes. Amen.

XXXI. Lives of the Saints

By faith Abraham, when God tested him, offered Isaac as a sacrifice. He who had embraced the promises was about to sacrifice his one and only son, even though God had said to him, "It is through Isaac that your offspring will be reckoned." Abraham reasoned that God could even raise the dead, and so in a manner of speaking he did receive Isaac back from death.

By faith Isaac blessed Jacob and Esau in regard to their future.

By faith Jacob, when he was dying, blessed each of Joseph's sons, and worshiped as he leaned on the top of his staff.

By faith Joseph, when his end was near, spoke about the exodus of the Israelites from Egypt and gave instructions about his bones.

Hebrews 11:17–22

It's an interesting story, with an ironic and most blessed twist. In Sant'Angelo Lodigiano, Italy, on July 15, 1850, Frances Cabrini was born two months premature, the tenth of her parents' eleven children, only four of whom lived past adolescence.

Perhaps it was her being premature, but throughout her life, Frances Cabrini, who would become Mother Cabrini, was sickly, so much so that church authorities doubted whether she had the wherewithal to become a "religious" (that's traditional Roman Catholic language). That's why, for instance, when she made application she was, each time, denied admission. No one doubted her faith; many doubted her stamina.

In 1863, having graduated from a training school for teachers run by the Daughters of the Sacred Heart, and having then petitioned that order for admission, she was, once again, refused. The authorities, once again, doubted her toughness.

Some say that to soften the blow of her rejection, the Mother Superior, who never doubted the adequacy of Cabrini's stout faith, told her that she was "called to establish a new Institute to bring glory to the heart of Jesus."

That was sweet. It was also prophetic.

Frances Cabrini, who became Mother Cabrini, did just that, sickly or not. When she died, at 67 years old, in Chicago, Illinois, Mother Cabrini had established 67 missions of mercy by way of the Institute she had established. Mother Cabrini was the very first American canonized by the Roman Catholic Church.

When Mother Teresa was awaiting the church's verdict on the mission she was sworn to create in a vision, she read – she likely devoured – the life of Mother Cabrini. "She did so much for the Americans because she became one of them," she wrote the Archbishop in a note. "Why can't I do for India what she did for [America]?" (47).

Protestantism's gift to political theory is and was the republicanism that arose from a theology that valued the idea of our being "saved by grace." Luther and Calvin and the others refused to believe that the church and its decrees or practices stood between God and the believer. In the Protestant view, access to God almighty is neither created nor regulated by the church. All men and women are created equal.

Well, mostly.

Don't get me wrong – this lifelong Protestant isn't petitioning the next synod to canonize our spiritual giants. Nope. But the lives of the saints have done marvelous things in the Roman Catholic world, served as models to help millions believe in their own consecration.

Whether or not Mother Teresa would have succeeded without the witness of the life of Mother Cabrini is a question not really worth asking. What we know is that Mother Cabrini's witness bore fruit in the life of a young idealist from Albania, a young teacher confident in a divine way that she'd heard directly from the voice of the Lord.

The lives of the saints, Protestant and Catholic, those canonized and those only quietly admired because so gloriously blessed – all of them enrich us, enrich our own lives.

PRAYER: Lord, thank you for the lives of the saints. Refresh our parched souls with stories of those whose witness shines in the darkness. Make us readers and remember-ers. Treat us with grand stories of faithfulness. Amen.

XXXII. Guilt or Whatever

"Love the Lord your God with all your heart and with all your soul and with all your mind and with all your strength." Mark 12:30

The very first Dutchman I ever met – I mean, someone from the Netherlands – told me that my people, Dutch Calvinist Americans, were the kind of uptight people Holland "got rid of," the kind, he said, who couldn't ride bikes on Sunday.

I couldn't ride my bike on Sunday.

My people were Sabbatarians, big-time Sabbatarians, a word my spell checker doesn't recognize. What I mean is, I had a list as long as my arm of things I couldn't do on the Sunday. We were orthodox Jews in wooden shoes, although we nailed down the first day of the week, not the last.

I don't regret my religious childhood. It may well have been, well, strenuously spiritual, but that's okay. Besides, most people my age – Catholic, Lutheran, Presbyterian, Church of Christ – had their own firmly established principles of right and wrong, a code, often only vaguely understood, by which they, as believers, defined themselves.

Many reasons exist to explain why my people were strict on Sunday (my mother-in-law couldn't use a scissors), and piety was one of them; but another, I think, was identity. Maintaining Sabbath purity separated us even from other Christians and allowed a good heavy dose of assurance about who we were in a polyglot society where you couldn't count on your neighbor having a pocket full of peppermints.

Codes sustain identity – I know something of who you are if I understand how you spend your Sundays. But to know thyself, as honorable as that is (saith Socrates), also implies knowing who isn't you – and knowing (tsk, tsk) what isn't, well, proper. If I know what the word *impropriety* means, it suggests I know guilt.

Guilt, Garrison Keillor says, is the gift that goes on giving, and I'm as much an unhappy recipient as anyone. Up until July, I was the only member of my family who went to two Sunday services, even though we were all raised that way. I've now decided enough is enough. Sound impressive? – come six o'clock Sunday night, I'll be hiding somewhere, not from others, but from my own thorny guilt.

More confession: I feel guilty when I read what Mother Teresa told the Archbishop in a letter begging him to allow her to create the mission that Christ himself, she claimed, had commanded her to do. "I have been longing to be all for Jesus and to make other souls – especially Indian, come and love Him fervently," she wrote, "– to identify myself with Indian girls completely, and *so love Him as He has never been loved before*" (47, emphasis mine).

Striking, I think – really striking: "So love Him as He has never been loved before." I find that a gargantuan mission. If I honestly didn't believe her a saint, I'd think it was posturing, wouldn't you? Rhetoric. Talk, talk, talk. How can anyone really believe that he or she will gain a level of love for Jesus that no one – NO ONE! – in the history of mankind has ever reached?

I don't envy her. I don't think I'd ever, ever say anything like that, and yet I believe that in life and in death, in body and soul, I belong to Jesus. Okay, I feel a species of guilt scratching at my throat when I read that line because it's something I'd never ever considered – that *my* love for Jesus might possibly be greater than anyone else's. I've never aspired to become the Champion of the World in love for Christ.

But she thought so, and, I believe, she thought so purely.

Here and there MT's writings suggest what she was made of and how what she was made of nurtured her into what she became. Right here is one such moment. The pledge she sets for herself is way beyond reason: to "so love Him as He has never been loved before."

Yet, I don't doubt her. Okay, I doubt myself most every day, but I don't doubt her.

Amazing.

PRAYER: Thank you for her words, Lord – thank you for a commitment that continues to brighten our lives through the years that have passed since she left this world. Bless us with commitment. If it can't be like hers, strengthen us anyway for the tasks you've blessed us with. Help us be as bold as she in the way we give away our love. In Jesus' name, Amen.

XXXIII. "THE HOLES OF THE POOR"

Carry each other's burdens, and in this way you will fulfill the law of
Christ. Galatians 6:2

"Come, come, carry Me into the holes of the poor." (44)

I must admit that if I were Christ's English prof, I'd suggest he find
some alternative to "the holes of the poor," language he used, says Mother
Teresa, when he told her about the new mission he had for her, language
which, these days, to say the least, lacks political correctness. *Holes* makes
the poor seem like pocket gophers – moles maybe, or, worse, rats. "Think
of the image you're creating," I might say, professorially.

But some history is in order. If in your imagination, you see Mother
Teresa's work among the poor the way I do, the backdrop is a U.S. slum
landscape, circa 1980 or so. Think Chicago, New York, LA. But Calcutta
in the 1940s was a slum of wholly different magnitude.

In the Great Famine of 1942 and 1943, somewhere between two
and four million people – I'm spelling those words so you don't think
them typos – died on Bengal streets for reasons that are, trust me, still
hotly debated and more than fiercely remembered. Two and four *million*
people. Chicago's population, in total, in 1940 was 3,400,400. Consider
them gone.

Once the Second World War ended, the battle for Indian independence from England resumed mightily until the British partitioned the
country into India *and* Pakistan, one predominantly Hindu, the other
Muslim, on Partition Day in August of 1947. At the very heart of the liberation movement *and* the division between national religions sat Bengal
and its central city, Calcutta.

National pride and religious hatred notwithstanding, there is no
way to describe what happened in Calcutta in August of 1946, just a year
before Partition Day, other than sheer madness. For four days and four
nights Muslims slaughtered Hindus, and Hindus slaughtered Muslims
in a holocaust of religious madness called today, "the Week of the Long
Knives." Exactly how many people died is almost anyone's guess – hundreds, thousands.

In September of that year, 1946, just two weeks or so after "the

Week of the Long Knives," Mother Teresa heard Jesus' voice on the train and at the retreat at Darjeeling. She was cloistered, of course, a teacher in a girls school; but she had to know that just outside those religious walls, hell itself had come to earth.

But there's more. In the time that surrounded Indian and Pakistani liberation from English rule, the time of national independence, the largest migration of population in the history of the world was taking place, millions of Hindus leaving their homes in Pakistan to take refuge in what would become Hindu India – and millions of Muslim Indians leaving their homeland for refuge in what would become Muslim Pakistan. Millions became homeless and hungry, and right there at the heart of the suffering once more was Calcutta.

The hungry of Calcutta

I don't claim to know what kind of language Jesus uses in his interlocutions, and I certainly don't know what's appropriate for the Savior of Mankind, if and when he speaks to any of us, to you or to me.

But because I know some history, I am not about to critique the language Mother Teresa claims he used to tell her he was calling her to service to the poor, right in their very "holes," because the world she saw and experienced outside the fortress of the school and convent where she lived was a suffering place unlike anything I can imagine.

The patio door is open now, and a beautiful breeze is coming into my study. It'll get hot soon once again, and I'll have to close it all up to keep the sun out, temperatures arising. The truth is, I know absolutely nothing about the suffering Mother Teresa saw every day on the streets of Calcutta – absolutely nothing in my life comes anywhere close.

When he told Mother Teresa to go to "the holes of the poor," he used language that couldn't possibly have made the situation more horrible than it actually was. She must have known something of that herself. All that suffering came to her as the voice of the Lord, horror and death happening daily all around.

In 1975, Paul Theroux wrote of Calcutta, "The city seemed like a corpse on which the Indians were feeding like flies." That was 30 years after Mother Teresa heard the Lord tell her to go to the poor, the ones who lived in holes. The task was not just daunting, it was impossible – without faith.

PRAYER: To some of us, the really privileged, the toll of human suffering in this world is unimaginable. Words or pictures can't describe it, Lord, but we know that somehow you are there. You're in the holes, in the caves, in the dugouts, the hovels. You are there. Give us means by which to go there too, to bring your love – and find it. In Jesus' name, Amen.

XXXIV. Giveaway

So Abram said to Lot, "Let's not have any quarreling between you and me, or between your herders and mine, for we are close relatives. Is not the whole land before you? Let's part company. If you go to the left, I'll go to the right; if you go to the right, I'll go to the left." Genesis 13:8–10

The preacher at the church we're attending since we've moved a month ago seems to me to be awfully young; but then, because I'm now retired, most do. He started, last week, a series on generosity, he said, assuming, I guess, that most of us need a spike in our giving. I don't doubt that we do, all of us.

I wanted to tell him about the Yankton Sioux, who were right here on this prairie long before any paleface showed up on what once was an ocean of grass – the Dakota, a tribe of people we worked hard to convert, a people who practiced "the giveaway" ritually (which is to say "religiously"), before we put them on reservations and told them giving away their meager fortunes was a heathen practice and outlawed it.

Most tribes in the Sioux family practiced "the giveaway" at significant moments in their lives, a kind of garage sale with one major exception: instead of dumping the clothes our toddlers have grown out of or an 8-track stereo, they gave away their best – their horses, their buffalo robes, their bead work. Their best. Get that. Their best. Didn't sell it either. Gave it away.

A Lakota Giveaway

Reputations were made or broken – one's standing in the community was created – by how much one gave away to those not blessed. Leaders became so by their sheer largesse. Bank accounts didn't cut any mustard among the Dakota; compassion marked character.

These people were plain heathen.

A young Albanian woman named Agnes Gonxha Bojaxhiu became Mother Teresa because of commitment *and* character, I suppose, or nature and nurture. But the heart of her commitment was something in her soul that made it impossible not to think royally of those, all of those, who weren't royally blessed.

In her book, *Mother Teresa: The authorised biography*, Navin Chawla quotes from someone she'd interviewed, someone with whose family Mother Teresa had stayed for some time. This man, Michael Gomes, told Chawla that once upon a time Mother Teresa had told him, "I feel it very deeply that I should be snug in my bed and that on the road there should be those who have no cover. I think it is wrong not to share."[1]

Mother Teresa saw more terrifying squalor than most of us will ever see – or want to. What she saw and experienced on the streets of Calcutta was, to me, unimaginable. Certainly the depth of suffering all around her created the spirited need to act.

But you can't help wondering, too, just how much of her commitment was generated by, first of all, her own character and, just as importantly, her commitment to be someone who has loved Jesus "as no one has loved Him before."

"I'd rather have Jesus than silver or gold." Richard Mouw used to say that as a Christian community we'd all be better off if we really believed the words we sing. I think he was right – of me, too.

But then, the American dream isn't all about giveaways, tribal rituals we made illegal because, after all, those savages had to learn how to get along in a glorified world of private property, where mine is mine.

When you read about MT's almost instinctive commitment to serve, I can't help but think we believers would do ourselves a great favor by giving away t-shirts plastered full of some of her most memorable statements, like this one: "I think it is wrong not to share."

Maybe we ought to sell them at the political conventions, where we'd likely lose our shirts.

Still, it's some ethic isn't it? – "I think it is wrong not to share."

---

1   Navin Chawla, *Mother Teresa: The authorized biography* (Boston: Element, 1992/1998), 20. A references to this book are included between {brackets}.

PRAYER: Give us a willing heart to serve, to give away, to share, Lord. It is, in many ways, the most pointed command you've given us in your Word; but it remains, for most of us, the most difficult thing to do. Thank you for the witness of Mother Teresa, whose life is a model. Fill our hearts with your love. Amen.

XXXV. Mystery

The word of the LORD came to Jonah son of Amittai: "Go to the great city of Nineveh and preach against it, because its wickedness has come up before me."

But Jonah ran away from the LORD and headed for Tarshish. Jonah 1:1–3

Years ago, I had a student, a young woman, who was embarrassingly, even incorrigibly shy. When I was a student myself, I hated being ambushed by a teacher – "Say, Schaap, what are the three earmarks of Renaissance poetic sentiment?" Duh.

"Do unto others" – and all that, right? So I didn't bushwhack students once I got on the other side of the desk.

But this student – I could tell by her mannerisms – was terminally shy. She'd sit in the back corner and hide for most of the class. She was no superstar academically, but neither was she a dolt; she did well. But it seemed to me that, at least in class, she prayed to be sheer.

I saw her at a ballgame one night – in the pep band. She was banging a drum. Seriously, of all things, she was a drummer! And she was good, even featured. That person with those sticks in her hands was someone completely other than the reserved little slip of a girl in the classroom's dark back corner.

One of the earmarks of good writing – or so it seems to me – is surprise, within reason. Great stories never end exactly where you thought they would – they surprise us. If they don't, we don't care. Great characters always surprise us, as do, often, almost all human beings.

We had a preacher once upon a time, a man I knew in college as being especially acerbic – witty but capable of cutting someone up like a dill pickle. When he accepted the call to be our preacher – something I voted for, by the way – I would have bet it wouldn't be more than six months before he'd offend someone with something he said.

He left a dozen years later, totally loved, not an alienated member in sight, all of them in tears at his departure. I'm still shocked.

There's a story about Mother Teresa that is similarly surprising. Father van Exem – her spiritual advisor, the priest to whom she went immediately after hearing Jesus' command to her to go out into the ghettos of Calcutta and be his hands – told his superior about a vision one of the sisters had, told him of the fiery directness of Jesus' voice to the young woman (he didn't disclose her name), told that superior that she'd heard that voice time and time again during the retreat at Darjeeling and that it wasn't just a dream that glanced off her consciousness. It was a voice, the voice of Christ.

Father van Exem's superior was a man named Father Henry, who, along with Van Exem, was Belgian. In fact, they were friends, close friends, since they'd entered the priesthood.

When Father Henry heard the news, he prayed and prayed and prayed, in part, one can imagine, because he too knew that the need was immense in the neighborhood where they lived. *Immense*, as in *gargantuan*. Father Henry wanted the vision to be sound and wanted the mission to be granted. He started praying immediately.

Later – significantly later, when the whole story came out and the sister who'd had the vision was identified – Father Henry learned from Father van Exem that the petitioner was none other than Mother Teresa, that little slip of a woman.

Father Henry was stupefied. He said no matter how he'd have tried, he would never guessed that the woman with the vision, the woman with the call, the woman recruited by Jesus Christ and given divine orders was Mother Teresa. Almost shocking.

Jesus Christ himself was the greatest mystery – how can a man be a god? How can a god be a man?

But we are his image-bearers, and it's helpful to remember that we too are capable of things we've never believed, things we've never attempted, things we've never guessed were in our powers to achieve.

Really, in each and every one of us there's a drummer.

Who would have guessed it would be little Mother Teresa? No one. But she heard and she listened, and she wouldn't stop banging on the door until what she believed she'd been told to do simply got done.

We're mysteries – all of us. And it's a blessing.

PRAYER: You've created us to be capable of great things, Lord, but sometimes our plain and simple humanness doesn't believe it. To know that Mother Teresa surprised the priests is to understand that any of us can. Give us grace to be your hands and feet in this world with its holes and its reoccurring sadnesses. Make us instruments of your peace. Amen.

XXXVI. Patience

I remain confident of this: I will see the goodness of the LORD in the land of the living. Wait for the LORD; be strong and take heart and wait for the LORD. Psalm 27:13–14

When it comes right down to it, only Peter left the skiff that night Christ invited all of his disciples to walk on water. Only Peter.

If Peter is the model of Christian obedience – okay, he sank, but at least he got up and out of that little fishing boat – then count me among the other 11, who likely took one look at the deep water and wondered if the supplicant voice they were hearing belonged to the Master or some guy in a mask. I admit it – I wouldn't have left the boat.

And that may well by why I feel such sympathy for Archbishop Ferdinand Périer, the Archbishop of Calcutta and head of the Archdiocese. Here's the story he heard from Father van Exem, MT's spiritual advisor: a slight and thin member of the Sisters of Laredo, a woman only recently, in 1944, made principal of the St. Mary's, a high school in Calcutta, has seen a vision, a series of them, in fact.

Fine. And what did that vision – those visions – ask of Mother Teresa?

Van Exem likely cleared his throat. That she quit the school and minister to the poor on the streets of the city.

Abandon her vows?

Well, alter them significantly so that she can go to the poorest of the poor and bring them, ah, love.

Now if I were Archbishop Périer, I might reach for coffee just then, or do something to bless the room with the kind of silence such a request created.

According to her biographer, Navin Chawla, Father van Exem, who entertained no insignificant amount of cynicism about Mother's request himself, insisted that this woman's interlocution was definitely to be believed. "Your grace," he said, "it is the will of God. You cannot change the will of God" {23}.

That's what's called "playing the God card." I can only imagine the look on the Archbishop's face. He was not particularly interested, I'm sure, in being spiritually blackmailed by an underling or an overly pious nun, and now Van Exem had upped the ante.

Now what must remembered at this dramatic moment in the story of Mother Teresa's life is that the ministry at which she became famous had not yet begun, wasn't in planning, was nothing but a vision, a command, as she adamantly maintained, from none other than Jesus Christ. It was, after all, his voice she'd heard. Of that fact, she harbored absolutely no doubt, even if others had and would.

Archbishop Périer must have worn a slightly twisted sneer. "I am the Archbishop," he said, "and I do not know the will of God, and you, a young priest in Calcutta, you know the will of God the whole time" {23}.

I swear, I could have said that, would have, in fact – "be reasonable!" Father van Exem was asking permission to allow a tiny little bird-like woman to go scavenging on the cut-throat streets of Calcutta, by herself, charged with the outrageous mission of befriending the poor, gazillions of them, being nice, bringing Christ's love.

The Archbishop knew it was just a matter of time before England gave India its independence, and no one – no one on earth – knew what that action would trigger between Bengal's warring religious factions. No one could have predicted the mass migration of people across what became national borders or that the starvation would only grow worse.

The Archbishop instructed Mother Teresa not to speak about her visions or plans with anyone, then waited a year to rule, the very year of Indian independence.

And then, finally, he said yes. I understand what was going on in his mind. I've got more than a touch of Doubting Thomas.

Our preacher liked to say – and often too – God seems to like to work very, very slowly. What Mother Teresa knew, even though she was absolutely sure she was at that moment disobeying the very voice of Jesus when *not going* to "the holes of the poor," was that patience was required – painful, never-ending, turtle-like patience.

PRAYER: Forgive us, Lord, when we begin to think that you're not doing our will. Forgive us for expecting change in our time, when eternity is the world in which you operate. Bless us with an understanding that isn't created by the clock, but by eternity. Give us patience to endure because we know your promises are sure. Amen.

XXXVII.
To Be Near Unto God

But as for me, it is good to be near God.
I have made the Sovereign LORD my refuge;
I will tell of all your deeds. Psalm 73:28

I've often wondered why God almighty points out King David as the human being closest to his heart. I'm sure theologians and academics have answers, but I've always speculated that the answer lies in his poems, the psalms, because even when he wasn't connected (see Psalm 13), he was.

King David constantly went to God, constantly. Angry, thrilled, celebrative, envious, depressed, jubilant, unsure of himself, quizzical, thankful, joyous, or incensed – he carried all of that up to God as if Jehovah was more than a confessor or best friend or marriage partner, as if he were, in fact, God.

Here's my speculation, take it or leave it: God loved King David – an adulterer, a murderer, a man with more moods than the moon – because David simply wouldn't NOT talk to him. No man was ever closer to God's heart because no man so consistently lugged his life's baggage – its glories and his humiliations – to the Lord.

One more little story about Mother Teresa's year of waiting. You may remember that, once she heard Jesus' voice on the way to and during the retreat at Darjeeling, once she was sure herself that the voice could not be anyone but Christ, she returned to the school where she was principal and told Father van Exem what she heard, who then brought the matter to the Archbishop, who, like Van Exem initially, couldn't help doubt the whole spiritual thing.

What's more, the idea was unimaginable – that this tiny lady hanging out on the dreadful streets of Calcutta, a place where suffering and poverty and blood came in torrents? – it was nigh unto insane. What's more, she was, after all, reneging, after a fashion, on her own vows to the Sisters of Laredo. The request was simply lunatic.

Yet, they all conceded to the proposition so that – even if it had taken a long, long time – she was granted permission. And here's what happened.

August, 1948. Father van Exem is given the esteemed privilege of breaking the news to his spiritual mentee. He celebrates mass that day, then catches Mother Teresa quickly and asks her to stay behind when the rest of the Sisters departed.

She did, sensing – those who knew her say – that finally, at long last, an answer was forthcoming. It had been Christ's own voice after all, Jesus speaking directly to her.

Father van Exem had mentioned that he had something to tell her, and when the two of them stood there together, she's the one who speaks, not him, even though he's the one with the news.

"Excuse me, Father," she tells him. "I will pray first" {26}.

There. That's David, bringing absolutely everything – his fears, his joys, his excitement. She brought it all to the Lord.

One more thing, as much a delight.

Father van Exem tells her that a reply from Rome had been received and her wish and her prayer was granted.

Immediately, she said, "Father, can I go to the slums now?"

Immediately. First crack out of the box.

She was ready.

Praise the Lord.

PRAYER: Make us ready to talk, Lord. Keep us in communication. Help us stay close to you, near as a neighbor and closer. Stay beside us, and keep us beside you. Amen.

XXXVIII.
THE WARDROBE OF THE LORD

Through him we received grace and apostleship to call all the Gentiles to the obedience that comes from faith for his name's sake. And you also are among those Gentiles who are called to belong to Jesus Christ. Romans 1:5–6

". . . your vocation is to love and suffer and save souls and by taking this step you will fulfill My Heart's desire for you. . . . You will dress in simple Indian clothes or rather like My Mother dressed – simple and poor." (48)

Thus saith the Lord. Seriously.

The quote above includes the exact words Mother Teresa claimed she heard Jesus tell her when he, startlingly, directed her to live among the poor, *with* them, *as* them. Even in dress. Gone would be the almost sacred habit, in its place the rags of Calcutta's poor.

Some men my age wear shorts to church these days – you know, the ones with baggy pockets. I can excuse such dress in those 30-somethings who believe that worship should be a picnic. But in older men – those who remember the "Sunday clothes" of their boyhoods – I guess I just don't understand. I'm no grumpy old fogy, by the way; I haven't worn a suit for years. But fall is coming, and, sooner or later, I'll get out a sport coat. No ties, however – good night, I'm not a museum piece.

There are practices with which I was brought up that I find difficult to break – like going to church twice on Sunday. We've been "oncers" now for a couple of months, and I rather like it, although I'm still not sure, as my father would say, that what I do with the time I'd otherwise be in church is as important, as selfless as worship.

Someday, when I depart this vale of tears, I'll still have "Sunday clothes" in the closet. The penchant to dress up for worship is in a vault of my subconscious, for better or for worse. If we had a meeting with our State Senator, my father used to say, we wouldn't wear swimming suits. Hard as this is to admit, I've got a thing about Sunday clothes, a thing that's not easily broken. But I'm on the other side of the Reformation, and I'm a thorough-going Protestant who grew up, terribly prejudiced, sometimes referring to nuns as penguins.

But what if I wasn't? What if, to me, the wardrobe of the Lord was the habit that I was born and reared adoring? What if my commitment to Jesus Christ and Mother Mary was quietly proclaimed in the white coif, the black veil, the rosary, the woolen belt, the holy habit and scapular? How hard would it be then, to remove them for something else?

I'm guessing only Christ himself could have persuaded Mother Teresa to change clothes. Only the voice of the Lord as she heard it could have demanded she step out of centuries of Roman Catholic tradition and piety in exchange for the rags of Calcutta's poor.

And he did, or so she heard him say.

So commanding was his voice, so determined was her obedience. Leave the habit behind, Sister. That's what he told her.

And she did. That's something, isn't it?

PRAYER: Give us ears to hear your voice, Lord, and grant us sufficient selflessness to obey. The penchant for going our own way is as old as the Garden. Bless us with grace to become your obedient servants in this world. Amen.

XXXIX. Conviction

Now faith is confidence in what we hope for and assurance about
what we do not see. Hebrews 11:1

Some historians claim that the unparalleled success of the Plymouth
and Massachusetts Bay Colonies in this new world, way back in early 17th
century, is directly attributable to the people's unsullied conviction that
they were – as none other – the children of God and that their coming to
this new land was nothing less than their obedience to his call. At Plymouth, half the immigrants were dead when the first spring came around,
but what stayed convincingly alive though all that horror was their faith
that the Creator of Heaven and Earth was behind them all the way.

Conviction creates results. The little engine that could, did. If you
honestly don't believe you can win the 1600 meters, you may as well hike
back up into the stands. As I write, the Rev. Robert H. Schuller is in a
nursing home, but for decades he chatted with Presidents and princes
largely because of the creed he carried, defiantly, into life itself – the sheer
power of positive thinking. Sadly, such faith hasn't kept him out of the
Home.

No matter – the man's gospel is at least half-truth, and nothing less
than the American dream is ready witness. Look at the young Ben Frank-
lin, poor as a church mouse, walking into Philadelphia with little more
than a couple of dimes. Look at Barack Obama, son of a single mom who
was, more often than not, on the other side of the world when he was a
kid. Yet her son somehow graduates from Harvard Law and becomes the
first African-American President of these United States. The American
Dream is molded from faith, conviction.

The very soul of Mother Teresa's plea to start a new mission en-
terprise on the streets of Calcutta was communication she claimed to
receive from none other than Jesus, who told her, in no uncertain terms,
to "come be my light" on the streets in "the holes of the poor."

Here's the way her biographer summarizes it: "Mother Teresa's certitude of being called by God and her desire to do His will gave her the
courage to persist." And more, "To ignore or deny this call would make
her guilty before God" (102).

Such certitude is a marvelous blessing. It's enabling, a divine resource to which nothing can compare. Conviction – certitude – is the very engine of our actions. So convinced was she of her Savior's voice that non-compliance was not an alternative. What we'd like to say is that she gained her dream because she simply couldn't *not* do so.

I don't know about you, but I can't help but envy, in a way, that kind of certitude, even though I doubt – there's the word, *doubt* – I'll ever have it. Let's just say it again – certitude is a marvelous blessing.

But so is cynicism. So is doubt.

There were moments in Mother Teresa's life when her conviction of God's voice went far beyond whatever doubt she might have harbored. In the year that followed those first commands she heard from none other than Christ himself, a year in which her immense conviction grew exponentially, she must have felt herself almost impossibly close to God.

But then, there were also moments when she was surely convicted that God had decided that he simply wasn't speaking to her, that he'd abandoned her; there were moments, many of them, when she heard no voice at all, when all she could see before her was the empty darkness.

There's a certain beauty in those extremes – the ecstasy and the agony. There's an undeniable humanness that, as far as I'm concerned, makes Mother Teresa even more of a saint. She was, after all, not all that far from you or me or the guy on the bus in front of us.

What separates her from just about anyone is her faith, but what makes her undeniably human is the plain fact that that immense and billowing faith, that foundational faith that enabled her to accomplish everything she believed Jesus Christ had commanded of her, sometimes also abandoned her, left her in tears of doubt and darkness. We'll see much more now. Beware.

Still, all that darkness makes her conviction, at least to me, even more of a blessing.

PRAYER: Lord God almighty, thank you for the blessing of conviction, the gift of faith, the light in the darkness, the very real substance of grace. Give us the strength of our convictions so that we know you are there with us, a single pair of footprints along the shores of our lives. And when the darkness comes, always help us see. In your name, Amen.

XL. NOTHING

For I am convinced that neither death nor life, neither angels nor demons, neither the present nor the future, nor any powers, neither height nor depth, nor anything else in all creation, will be able to separate us from the love of God that is in Christ Jesus our Lord.

Romans 8:38–39

Seriously?

The Apostle Paul's searing claim is, in some ways, characteristic of the zealot he always was. Absolutely *nothing* will separate us from God's love in Christ? Nothing? Seriously?

It may be difficult to locate another single line of scripture that so boldly proclaims the sovereign character of God's love as Paul's in this chapter from the letter to the Romans – nothing, absolutely nothing can pull us away from God's love. Nothing.

The Bible's poetic character carries along more than its share of hyperbole or overstatement. Give Paul a break here – he's just really pumped and people sometime mumble extravagant things when they are. Take it with a grain of salt, eh?

My very pious great-great-grandfather came to America in the 1840s, got himself a chunk of land outside a pioneer community called Milwaukee, Wisconsin. Then, in a matter of just a year or so, lost three sons and his wife to some vile, rampaging disease. I'm sure he spoke no English; he was just off the boat, really, a citizen of a brand new, barely understandable world. After suffering that kind of loss, I wonder whether he felt separated from God's love. Even Job did, after all.

Still, it's there, isn't it? – Paul's bravura. Even if you've heard that line only once, it will stick to the memory like eternity. Nothing. Nothing at all can separate us from his love.

When the church finally granted Mother Teresa the calling she claimed Jesus himself demanded of her – to go into the darkest, dankest dens of human suffering in the city around her – Mother Teresa faced a difficult problem: she believed she would have to leave the Order. Part of the call Jesus gave her was to *become* the poor, not just to be like the poor in their Calcutta hovels, but to *be* them; and that divine directive meant leaving the Sisters of Loreto and breaking the vows she'd made 18 years before. In order to follow Christ, she would have to undergo a separation the church itself called "secularization."

But she was resolute.

> Nobody can unbind me from God – I am consecrated to Him and as such I desire to die. – I don't know what the Canon Law has to say in this matter – but I know Our Lord will never allow Himself to be separated from me. – Neither will He allow anyone to separate me from Him. (87)

That's what she wrote in a letter to her spiritual mentor, that's the pledge she gave him, not as if to assuage his fear but to proclaim as defiantly as she could that even in reneging on her vows she wasn't, for a moment, expecting even the slightest separation from the grace she'd always known. She was, in essence, willing to give up the church to follow Christ.

And she meant it. She wasn't playing politics or plying her superiors to get her way. What she claimed was not hyperbole or poetic license. Like Paul, she was totally convinced, completely convinced, that nothing would separate her from the Love of God, not height nor breadth nor angels nor demons, nor anything else in God's green earth or some spiritual world. Not death. Not life. Nothing. Absolutely nothing.

Seriously. Seriously.

PRAYER: Lord, give us faith like hers. Give us faith like Paul's. Give us faith to believe, no matter what our circumstance, that we are, all of us, the very beholden recipients of your own "blessed assurance." And thank you for Paul's words, and for Mother Teresa's – thank you for the gift of their deep faith. Amen.

XLI. PERSISTENCE

"And there was a widow in that town who kept coming to him with the plea, 'Grant me justice against my adversary.' For some time he refused. But finally he said to himself, 'Even though I don't fear God or care what people think, yet because this widow keeps bothering me, I will see that she gets justice, so that she won't eventually come and attack me!'" Luke 18:3–5

The famous judge in this famous parable is often called "the unjust judge" because, sadly enough, justice isn't his thing. His thing is peace – his own. Christ makes clear that this judge, who doesn't fear God, couldn't care less about justice. It's the widow's infernal nagging that moves him finally to act – the squeaky wheel gets the grease, we like to say.

Anyone who browses through the Mother Teresa story after her call to ministry among the poor can't help but get the sense that this woman – no widow and no child either – turned into the persistent widow of the parable, because Mother Teresa simply would not let her cause – the new dream ministry – alone. Clearly, she was on a crusade, leading it, in fact, right out there in front.

She'd passed the tests administered by Father van Exem, her spiritual counselor, and then (after waiting again, this time for an entire year) by those created by the Archbishop – and he was no slam dunk.

What remained was a judgment about the new mission Jesus commanded her to undertake, a judgment that would be rendered by Mother Gertrude, concerning the Loreto order with whom she was not only associated but bound, by oath. What she needed was a signal from her own Superior General as to how the new calling would look, on paper as well as in life.

Took a while. Too long. Way too long, thought Mother Teresa.

Impatient? – probably. Rash? – some might say so. Maybe just persistent, like the widow. So, should we call her *tireless* or *tiresome*? Maybe a little of both.

In her great haste, she sent off another letter to the Archbishop, hoping he would exercise his considerable power and push Mother Gertrude along. He may well have rolled his eyes a bit at her persistence, the sheer impatience of her unflagging spirit, so he begged her to remember that Mother Gertrude was likely busy.

"To have her answer now would suppose that she had nothing else to do but to write to you at once without reflection," he snapped in a letter. "Perhaps she was sick or in visitations." Then he offers a gentle bit of advice: "Take a little time. If Our Lord wishes to work miracles in this case certainly He can do it, but we have no right to expect them. . ." (112).

All of that translates easily into "Just take it easy."

But no one stands for long in the path of an Indo-Chinese tsunami, a Kansas tornado, or, I suppose, an Albanian nun who's been talking to Jesus (I'm sure she'd say *listening*.)

There's more to the parable, of course. How much more, Jesus says, will I grant justice when you call on the name of the Lord than this "unjust judge?" And I suppose that's the point finally, isn't it? Whether she was tireless or tiresome, what is most important about her persistent begging was her tireless and selfless devotion, not to her cause but to the work of the Holy Spirit among the poor in Calcutta. What she wanted was not that her will be done, but that God's be accomplished, that his own be loved.

And what God heard – I think – is her own grand and beautiful persistence to be his servant to his people in the "dark holes" of poverty she saw all around her.

"The art of love," a man named Albert Ellis once wrote, "is largely the art of persistence."

I like that, and I think Father van Exem would agree, as would Archbishop Périer, and Mother Gertrude as well. Even Mother Teresa.

"The art of love is largely the art of persistence."

PRAYER: In our commitments, Lord, make as steady as a rock. Give us the persistence of an ocean, the determination of nothing less than the wind itself. Thank you for the witness of a persistent widow whose cause was not her own but justice. Make us tireless advocates of your love. Amen.

XLII. Taking Note

Humble yourselves, therefore, under God's mighty hand, that he may lift you up in due time. 1 Peter 5:6

The crazy thing is, I can't remember selling the novel – but I must have. Somehow, my copy got into a used book bin, because years later a student in some university down South picked it up, required reading for a lit class she was taking. Faulkner, I think it was – maybe *As I Lay Dying*.

It's not my style to toss books that I've scribbled full of notes, and I'm sure I wrote in this one because I always do when I use a book of almost any kind in class. I'm sure this one was scored with gloss, a grand mess of underlinings, jots and tittles, and, I'm sure, a rainbow of bright, highlighted sentences.

Or so she said. This woman who became its recipient found me somehow at my college address and sent me an e-mail to thank me for all of my blessed notations. The scribbles, she said, helped her understand Faulkner's complex novel. She was thrilled with my notes.

I know scholars, literature scholars, who have spent years with original manuscripts, page by page, looking over typed lines a writer edited or reupholstered in finer language, noting changes in how the story's characters dress or act or speak. A manuscript's edits create their own stories.

The real reason people in my profession pour over dusty pages is the desire to understand the writer. Sometimes what gets edited or underscored or highlighted can be as revealing as what is actually typed on the page.

As it is in the very sweet letter Archbishop Périer sent to Mother Teresa when, like the persistent widow, she simply couldn't wait for Mother Gertrude to respond to her questions.

Here's how the kind Archbishop responded to her request to hurry the process:

> In due time the reply will come, remain quiet. Pray much and live intimately with Our Lord J.C. [Jesus Christ] asking for light, strength, decision; but do not anticipate HIS WORK. Try not to put anything of your own in all this. You are His instrument, nothing more. I do pray also, but I would be disappointed if perhaps things went too fast. (112)

A wonderfully pastoral letter.

That letter survives because Mother Teresa gave it to Father van Exem, telling him that he could destroy it when he finished reading because she had, she said, copied what she needed to know. When Father van Exem looked at the note, this is what he found:

> In due time the reply will come, remain quiet. <u>Pray much and live intimately with Our Lord J.C. asking for light, strength, decision</u>; but do not anticipate <u>HIS WORK. Try not to put anything of your own in all this. You are His instrument, nothing more.</u> I do pray also, but I would be disappointed if perhaps things went too fast.

Her underscoring what she did, the way she did – single underline, double underline – is as full of her character as anything she ever wrote herself. Look at what she noted, what she understood she had to remember, and you can feel her yet.

And she's there too in the way she explained all this to her mentor. "The letter is simply beautiful," she told him in a note. And then, "Pray for light that I may see and [for] courage to do away with anything of self in the work. I must disappear completely – if I want God to have the whole" (113).

Humility is a word whose origins are in *humus,* or the earth itself. In a paradox vastly more mysterious than I can explain or even understand, a seeming contradiction clearly observable in the life of Mother Teresa, her divine work in Calcutta could begin only on the ground, in the supine humility of the earth itself before her God.

(This is part of a prayer that Mother Teresa urged others to pray every day:)

PRAYER: O Jesus! meek and humble of heart, make my heart like unto Thine. From the desire to be esteemed, deliver me. . . . Jesus, grant me the grace to desire . . . to become as holy as I should that I might imitate the patience and obedience of Your mother, Mary. Amen.

XLIII. Pride

Pride brings a person low, but the lowly in spirit gain honor. Proverbs 29:23

This famous 16th century woodcut by Pieter Bruegel, one of a series based on the Seven Deadly Sins, features mirrors, lots of them, because the moral of story is all about pride. Ours.

Pieter Bruegel, "Pride" from *The Seven Deadly Sins*, 1556–1558

Human pride is often considered the first of what are traditionally called "the Seven Deadlies." Up front in the old Brueghel print is a woman admiring her reflection while simultaneously clutching something resembling a knife in her other hand. There is a monster in the center foreground who is so taken with himself that he admires even his nether parts. Yet another appallingly grotesque monster – human face, claw-like arms, and extended wings like a cicada-killing wasp – licks his chops delectably at his own image, offered to him by a strange nun-like woman who is gesturing magnanimously, her robe barely covering a reptilian tail.

There's more to the woodcut – believe me!

But then, I suppose, there's no end to the extent of human pride in all of us, pride that bowled over Eve first, then Adam, both of whom wanted *more*, despite the glory of Eden.

The English language has a thousand synonyms for pride, it seems. *Lordly* – see it? Or even more exotic, *baronial*. To be *proud* is to be *high-minded*, *high-mettled*, *high-handed*, *high-plumed*, *high-flown*, or *high-toned*. There's *arrogance*, *audacity*, *aloofness* – and we say of some over-bearing prigs that they're "putting on airs." What we feel when we're around them is *contempt*, *disdain* for the sheer *insolence* of their *pomposity*. Lots and lots of words.

I've said enough. The fact is, pride belongs not to *them*, to others, but to us, to all of us. The human condition, life after the fall, makes the cardinal rule of the Christian life – to love others more than we love ourselves – nigh unto impossible.

When her immediate superiors, one after another, gave Mother Teresa permission to leave the convent and follow Jesus' own voice in the slums of Calcutta, she was left with one more petition – to the Holy See. This is how she wrote Y.E. (Your Eminence):

> In all sincerity I admit that I possess no virtue and have no merit; it is a mystery to me how the Good God wants this from poor me. All these years of my religious life, I have been quite happy as a member of the Institute of the Bl. V.M. [Blessed Virgin Mary] and the thought of leaving it breaks my heart. Why Almighty God calls me now to this new life I do not know, but I want to do only His Holy Will without any reserve, whatever the cost be. (116)

I admit it. I find such abject humility hard to believe. We are – all of us – such bloody victims of pride that believing someone could actually expunge the most deeply-embedded sin of human mind and soul is almost beyond me.

But it's worth noting that believing Mother Teresa's *selflessness* was the required first step in the judgments made by each one of her superiors, from her mentor to the Holy See. They had to believe that there was no ego in her vision, no pride in the peculiar mission she was convinced she had been directed to by the very voice of Jesus.

And, not without some lingering doubts, not without some hesitation, they did believe her.

Along with her letter to the Holy See was a cover letter from the archbishop, who wrote a kind of recommendation for her and her unique petition. Among other things, he wrote, "I believe her to be," he said, "very mortified and very generous" (117).

Mortified – isn't that a ridiculous word? It's almost impossible for me to believe that anyone today would ever use that word to recommend someone else – "mortified."

Here's the rub. That descriptor, I'm sure, is probably exactly what the Holy See wanted to read. What's more, if you believe your Bible, it's what God wants – our mortification, the death of the old man of sin. Be ye mortified, the Bible might well say. Be ye *mortified*.

What God wants is impossible, isn't it? Humanly impossible, given our arrogance.

By grace alone.

PRAYER: It's nigh unto impossible for us to deny the legacy of Adam's fall, the pride we hold in placing ourselves forever first in whatever circumstance surrounds us. Forgive us for our egos. Grant us the mortification you demand, the mortification that only your grace can bring. In the name of your son, who gave himself for us. Amen.

XLIV. Holy Fools

The LORD is my strength and my shield; my heart trusts in him, and
he helps me. My heart leaps for joy, and with my song I praise him.

Psalm 28:7

When he left Grand Rapids, Michigan, he promised the powers-
that-be, the reigning potentates of the denomination he served, that he
would not only faithfully carry out the office of missionary, he'd also
continue to study so that he could – as he certainly should, they said –
eventually become a preacher.

That was a promise he broke. It would be interesting to know if he
ever intended to continue his seminary studies. What happened when
he came to New Mexico to bring the Word of Christ to the Navajo and
Zuni Indians became too all-consuming, and he never again opened a
schoolbook, which irritated – no, angered, even infuriated – the mission
board back east.

He was, after all, an unlikely missionary anyway. He knew Dutch,
of course, his native tongue – and Frisian, a whole different language
from his native Holland. And English, sort of. And the day he came to
Ft. Defiance, Arizona, he must have realized that doing mission work
among the native people required learning their languages too.

He wasn't dumb. One of
the first things he did was buy
the fastest horse he could, in
part because he understood
that a fast horse would be a
wonder to the natives – a white
man preacher on the fastest
horse in the territory was really
not to be believed.

He never studied a day
of anthropology, knew nothing about the Navajo's horror-
filled "Long Walk," had no
clue about the Zunis hiding up

Andrew and Effa Vander Wagen

on the mountain from the Spanish Conquistadors when they searched, in vain, for the Seven Cities of Gold. He knew very little about those he was about to serve.

But today there's a spot on the highway between Gallup and the Zuni pueblo, a place named VanderWagen, New Mexico. He and his wife, Effa, left a lasting mark on the whole region, even though as a young missionary he knew next to nothing about the world he was entering.

On August 17, 1948, Mother Teresa must have slipped out of the nun's habit she'd worn for decades, must have primped her hair slightly, and put on a sari with a blue border and taken to the streets of the city. She had this at least – she knew the world she was entering; after all, she'd served the Lord in Calcutta for more than a decade. She knew where she was and what her task consisted of.

But still, think of it this way: a deeply committed Albanian nun, more European than Indian, a woman sworn to follow Jesus, a woman with the voice of Christ still ringing in her ear, steps out of the habit *and* out of the convent that had been her only world since childhood, shuts the door behind her, dressed like an Indian, sworn to poverty, and begins a brand new life.

In the many mansions of God's own house, there are thousands of "holy fools," I'm sure, millions of true believers who weren't interested in listening to what was possible, but instead simply got up off their couches and stepped into commitments that may well have cost them their lives.

It is amazing what abiding faith can inspire.

Here's the whole truth: holy fools are not necessarily smart; but when they're authentic – when they're not wolves in sheep's clothing, my word! – they certainly are holy.

PRAYER: Trust and obey, for there is no other way to be happy in Jesus, but to trust and obey. Amen.

XLV. The School at Motijhil

"If you have faith as small as a mustard seed, you can say to this mulberry tree, 'Be uprooted and planted in the sea,' and it will obey you." Luke 17:6

After 20-some years with the Sisters of Lorato at the Entally Convent, after two years of waiting, sometimes impatiently, on the will of her superiors, after just four long months of medical instruction at Patna, Mother Teresa, dressed in what might well be considered a shoddy sari, the wardrobe of the poor, walked out into the streets of Motijhil, a place whose name translates "Pearl Lake," but, in 1948 at least, was anything but.

Today, guidebooks say, Motijhil is an almost middle-class suburb; but back then it was a *bustee*, a slum, a desolate place full of refugees from the starving countryside. India – and Calcutta specifically – was suffering through the after-effects of World War II, immense poverty and starvation, and a glut of country folks looking merely to stay alive in India's cities. People lived in shacks, had little food, and lacked the wherewithal to send their children to school. Motijhil was no "pearl lake"; the only source of water something putrid and sewage-filled. In 1948, Motijhil was infested with "the holes of the poor."

But ministering to the poor in those holes is what Mother Teresa claimed Jesus himself had called her to do, and, once ready and able, she walked into the world of hunger and sickness and starvation as if charmed by none other than the Holy Spirit.

From the local priest, she obtained the names of several families who made their often windowless homes in the neighborhood and told parents that she was about to start a school for refugee children right there within reach. Starting a school seemed without question the right alternative for her, having been a teacher herself for so long.

"Tomorrow," she must have told them. "Tomorrow, I will begin teaching."

That she had nothing – no blackboard or chalk, no slates, no pencils, no tablets, no books – seemed of little importance it seems. "Tomorrow," she must have said, "have your children there ready to learn."

That night, she returned to an old folks' residence maintained by the Little Sisters of the Poor. Likely as not, she lay awake for hours, dreaming of what was to come.

What was to come was peculiarly *her* dream, not the dream of most of us. Right there beside a stinking pool, right where she had directed those parents, the next morning, bright and early, she found five little children waiting for her.

So she started beneath a tree, this odd European woman in a third-rate sari and dusty sandals. "I took a stick and used it as a marker on the ground where the children sat," she told her biographer. "We began right on the ground" {34}.

Mother Teresa was no first-year teacher, and the children who showed up that day, on the first day of a school with a dirt floor, were not part of her first class. But somehow I can't help but think that, if she were still alive today, she could remember each of those five faces, each of the children who'd found their way to the school beneath the tree from the holes of the poor.

Somehow, I can't help thinking that that afternoon, after school, when Mother Teresa spent an hour or so walking back to the old folks' home where she was staying, she was praising God, praising God on high.

PRAYER: Blessed be your name, O Lord. Thank you for the testimony of those who love you, those who follow your direction in love and thanksgiving. Amen.

XLVI. Discipleship

If someone else thinks they have reasons to put confidence in the flesh, I have more: circumcised on the eighth day, of the people of Israel, of the tribe of Benjamin, a Hebrew of Hebrews; in regard to the law, a Pharisee; as for zeal, persecuting the church; as for righteousness based on the law, faultless. But whatever were gains to me I now consider loss for the sake of Christ. Philippians 3:4–7

He'd assembled, up there at the front of the church, a museum of memorabilia, buttons and medals and trophies, honors tassels from high school grad, two diplomas and a suitably framed preaching license, a couple decades' worth of accolades. This energetic young preacher, full of life and spirit, paraded us through his achievements with enough self-deprecation to make the trip humorous and memorable.

It was darlingly accomplished, but the whole demonstration was rhetorical because once he'd reviewed his own life's accomplishments – "best three-point shooter in junior high," etc. – he bashed the whole business, saying what Paul is saying in Philippians, third chapter, that all such hoopla is meaningless, that whatsoever we might achieve in life means total zero in light of the eternity of God's eternal love for us his own.

Memorably rhetorical, I'd put it. *Memorable* because it was really cute – a tongue-in-cheek recital of his own greatest hits, and *rhetorical* because it was a set up for the real punch line – "But whatever were gains to me I now consider loss for the sake of Christ."

"How many of us could say that?" he said, or words to that effect – that what we are, what we work for, what we want, our dreams and visions and desires – that all of that is less than zilch. How many of us would really give it all up for Christ?

He's a young kid, full of energy, capable of breaking eardrums in his spirited enthusiasm. The church loves him and that's wonderful.

But I think I've heard that sermon dozens of times before. What's more, I don't need a preacher to tell me that I care too much about what I do, about the very words I'm typing right now, the words you're reading – their order, their precision, their beauty. I care a ton about what happens on this page, and I care a ton about other things as well – about my kids, my grandkids.

Our attachment to this world isn't cheap or even transient, but I'm fully capable of asking myself, right now, whether these words are really worth my time, and – even more easily – whether the Green Bay Packers sweatshirt I just bought on e-bay (used!) is really something I needed or only something I wanted. The purpose of the sermon was to tell us to shape up our values, to align them with a confession of faith that places our love for the Lord above all else.

Here's Mother Teresa on the purpose of the new order she was creating for the poor: "The missionary must die daily, if she wants to bring souls to God. She must be ready to pay the price He paid for souls, to walk in the way He walks in search of souls" (140).

Same chapter and verse. Same sermon.

But somehow, given her story, the gospel truth bleeds from the words and the ideas those words create. Somehow, given how she lived, that "same old, same old" has currency beyond anything I could imagine or inflict on my own.

Don't get me wrong – that young preacher is wonderful, and there was nothing amiss in his sermon. But somehow, for me at least, reading those words from Mother Teresa creates a discourse that operates at a whole different level.

Honestly, I'm not indicting the preacher. He spoke the gospel.

But Mother Teresa really and truly lived it. She experienced death daily on the streets of Calcutta. She paid the price. She walked "in the way He walked in search of souls."

PRAYER: Help us never to grow callous to the gospel, never to answer questions before they're asked, to see the beckoning demands of a Christian life as simply rhetorical or cliché, Lord. And thank you for testimony, for the stories of those who have done what you beg us to do, to own up to the riches of your love by giving our own love away. Amen.

XLVII. UNDERSTANDING THE POOR

Whoever is kind to the poor lends to the LORD, and he will reward them for what they have done. Proverbs 19:17

By nature I suppose, I'm not someone given to making blanket generalizations. Life, to me at least, is too complicated, too many-cornered, too rife with paradox, seeming contradictions that in reality simply are not.

No matter. Here's one I dare make – every Christian believer understands the absolute importance of taking care of the poor, the voiceless, the powerless. Love is the great commandment, and that love is expressed most clearly in giving one's life for others. We all know that. No one can read the gospels – no one can read the Bible itself – and not know that Christ's teaching about the powerless is ever at the heart of things.

But here's the rub. How? – that's where the difficulty arises. Enter politics.

Tonight, two Presidential candidates, both of whom confess Jesus, will spar for 90 minutes on just that question. No one expects much agreement.

On February 16, 1949, Mother Teresa wrote this entry, redolent with character, in her diary.

> I went to meet the landlord of 46 Park Circus. The man never turned up. I am afraid I liked the place too much – and our Lord just wants me to be a "Free Nun", covered with the poverty of the Cross. But today I learned a good lesson – the poverty of the poor must be often so hard for them. When I went round looking for a home, I walked and walked till my legs and arms ached. I thought how they must also ache in body and soul looking for home, food, help. Then the temptation grew strong. The palace buildings of the Loreto came rushing into my mind. All the beautiful things and comforts – in a word, everything. "You have only to say a word and all that will be yours again," the tempter kept saying. Of free choice, My God, and out of love for you, I desire to remain and do whatever be Your Holy Will in my regard. I did not let a single tear come, even if I suffer more than now. I still want to do your Holy Will. This is the dark

night of the birth of our Society. My God give me courage now, this moment, to persevere in following your Will. {47}

This entry is not short on theological perception; after all, the tempter himself makes a skulking appearance. But what I find remarkable is MT's willingness to associate her own fears and anger that day with the perceived experience of those who daily suffer from the dishonor of broken promises, empty cupboards, and leaky roofs. Her own personal distress that day actually led her into considering anew the distress of others, those less fortunate. Instead of gathering her own spite into a fist, she reaches out for others, sees them more clearly in her own distress.

It's a gorgeous little story, really, a story she didn't mean to tell us; a story she simply recorded as her personal testimony after a very trying day.

Still, without a doubt, what happened that morning brought her closer to the poor and the destitute, the people she wanted to serve. Her empathy, amply demonstrated here, was the starting point for her mission, as it should be for all of ours.

PRAYER: Give us eyes wide open to those in need, wherever they are. Help us give empathy. Guide us in giving away our fish and our fishing poles. Help us best know how to love those who need love deeply. Give us your heart, Lord Jesus. Amen.

XLVIII. Treasure House

"Then the King will say to those on his right, 'Come, you who are blessed by my Father; take your inheritance, the kingdom prepared for you since the creation of the world.'" Matthew 25:34.

In Calcutta in the late 1940s, men and women and children were dying on the streets. Notice I said, "on" the streets, not "in" the streets. In some places and at some times, dying "in the streets" conjures images of insurrection, confrontation, and riotous civil strife. I meant to say what I did: in Calcutta, mid-century, men and women and children were dying on the streets – literally, *on* the streets.

They were human beings – men, women, and children – who were simply considered gone, those for whom the limited medical facilities had no room. They were dying, hopelessly alone, on the streets, corpses left at the side of the road.

Perhaps we should consider Mother Teresa and her Missionaries of Charity the very first hospice nurses in India, maybe even Asia, maybe even the world. What she couldn't help but see before her daily was not only death, but death without hope. Calcutta's city government gave her a place for the dying, a place she called "*Nirmal Hriday*," or "pure heart," in celebration of "the blessed virgin"; and *Nirmal Hriday* soon became a hospice center, a place that offered the dying poor at least a bit of what we call today "death with dignity."

Fifty years earlier, on the Navajo Reservation in the American southwest, Protestant missionaries from my own church found themselves besieged by death and dying. Traditionally, the Navajo people held the belief that the bodies of the dead were haunted by the evil spirits of death itself. Sometimes, if a death occurred in a hogan, the place would be burned. Navajos, traditionally, weren't so much afraid of death as they were horrified by it.

So they would bring their dead and dying to traders and missionaries, Anglos who would, graciously, dispose of those haunted bodies. Today the cemetery behind what was once the Rehoboth mission complex is still laden with unmarked graves of those dead and dying once long ago delivered to the mission hospital.

I don't doubt that taking up the burden of dealing frequently with the dead and dying, almost as if it were a service to the Navajo people, could be wearing and difficult, even expensive. But the missionaries did it. They took the role of peace-givers; and the case can be made, I believe, that had they not, they would never have secured the favor of the people they came to serve over the length and breadth of the sprawling Navajo reservation.

That blessed service – like Mother Teresa's – may well have met with only limited success in "conversions," in bringing lost souls home to the Lord. After all, blessing the dying with comfort may well have less to do with what we call "evangelism," than with simply giving away love. *Nirmal Hriday*, like those mission graves, is, or so it seems to me, what Matthew 25 is all about, the gift of love itself: when I was dying, you gave me a pillow.

Here's the way Brian Kolodiejchuk describes it, in *Mother Teresa: Come Be My Light:* "[At *Nirmal Hriday*] she and her sisters would bring the dying off the streets and offer them accommodation, basic medical care and above all, tender love" (145).

Maybe I read Matthew 25 poorly, but it seems to me that what Christ offers us in the little story of sheep and goats, right and left, is nothing more and nothing less than tender love.

PRAYER: Forgive our selfishness, Lord – forgive our preoccupation with self in the light of the suffering all around us. Prompt us, obediently and lovingly, to visit the sick, to clothe the naked, to shelter the homeless. Arm us, O Lord, with selfless, tender love in your name. Amen.

XLIX. Prayer Warriors

"Ask and it will be given to you. . . ." Matthew 7:7

At the beginning of his book *A Public Faith*,[1] Miroslav Volf describes what he calls an "active" faith, a faith that exists in a clear and vital relationship to our everyday lives, and begins by talking about the importance of "blessing," because, he insists (and we know), we always need it. Asking for it, however, can be off-putting and seem, sometimes, silly, as in praying for a fast pitch a kid can slam into the bleachers to bring home the winning run. You know – Tebow.

"Does God really care which team wins or what grade I get?" Volf asks.

What's worse, he says, enlisting God's help only on rare occasions may well turn us into Lance Armstrong types, using God almighty as if he were just another "performance-enhancing drug."

Okay, I admit it – I tend to think of Tebow-types as having a cheap view of how the Creator and sustainer of the universe relates to this world, as if God almighty were little more than a rocket booster. Besides, somewhere inside of me is the voice of Ralph Waldo Emerson, who insisted that leaning on the everlasting arms suggests we can't carry our own weight.

"The sophisticated among us sometimes dismiss such prayers," Volf says of people who roll their eyes at such "blessings," as if they were little more than passing fancies. Ouch. Count me among the pseudo-sophisticates. Way too often I roll my eyes.

But then Volf says – and he's no slouch, of course – "It is important to connect God with success in work." If for no other reason, he says, that's true because asking for blessing is vividly and consistently scriptural. What's more, God delivers. He does it. He *does* hand out blessings – this we know.

I'm not proud of my skepticism. I understand it. I can even attempt an excuse: I've been privy to too many well-meant prayers from too many people who should have – from my point of view – simply pulled

---

1 *A Public Faith: How followers of Christ should serve the common good* (Grand Rapids: Brazos, 2011), 25.

themselves up with their own bootstraps. Furthermore, if public praying wasn't fraught with the potential for hypocrisy, Christ himself wouldn't have told us to bring it into a closet, to make it private. See, I'm smart.

But then there's this – a note, just two days ago, from a friend, a good man in a battle with cancer, who claims that he can actually feel the mighty uplift of the prayers of his friends prayed a continent away, mine included.

And this: one of the first things Mother Teresa undertook as her new ministry began was to enlist a whole cadre of prayer warriors, every Sister having a "second self," a prayer partner whose duty it was, from afar, "to pray & suffer for her" (153). What she lined up with people both from the region and eventually the world was what she might have thought of as a circle of prayer, of pray-ers, who, like a fortress, bolstered the entire loving operation by, literally, suffering with them.

Especially important to her was the suffering of those prayer warriors. As her own team of prayer warriors, she wanted, and enlisted, "the paralyzed, the crippled, the incurables" – those who also were also suffering wherever they were; "second selves" specially recruited to, as she often said, "satiate the thirst of Christ."

This battalion of eternal reinforcements gave her great joy and those she served, she says, great comfort.

And me? I wonder if my own skepticism – my "sophistication," as Volf says – isn't simply created by way of the ease with which I've been blessed to live my life. In comparison with those forsaken thousands on Calcutta's streets – and even many of my friends – my own suffering has been barely worth mentioning.

What I know is that the day will come, as it does for each of us, the day I too will need friends, fellow sufferers, to storm the gates of heaven.

PRAYER: Thank you for a life bereft of suffering, Lord, but help me rid myself of the pride it requires to believe that we don't need you. We know better. Help us to pray. Amen.

L. Darkness (1)

I am overwhelmed with troubles and my life draws near to death.
I am counted among those who go down to the pit; I am like one
without strength. Psalm 88:3–4.

So the sermon yesterday was on worry, and the preacher was agin'
it. Like sin. It was the kind of sermon lifelong churchgoers like me could
have written ourselves, or at least outlined, once the scripture was read.
Same old, same old. Our old preacher used to say that "Fear not!" was
among, if not the greatest of all the commandments, at least the one most
repeated in scripture. I knew that.

Yet, we fear. Yet, we worry. Yet, we feel abandoned. Yet, we know
darkness. We're human, I guess, all of us.

Somewhere in *To Be Near Unto God*, Abraham Kuyper says that
those who are troubled by insomnia – which often means troubled by
something other than not sleeping – should learn, simply enough, to
take advantage of the night's long and empty spaces by reading, by doing
worthwhile stuff. Instead of just lying there worrying, he says, spend the
time in prayer or in the Word. Read a good book.

Abraham Kuyper taught me a great deal in that wonderful devotional book of his, but I remember that
advice particularly because it seemed to
fit under the category my college students would label "Duh," as in, "good
night, startlingly obvious."

I've said it before, and I must
admit it's an attribute of *Come Be My
Light* that drew me to the life of Mother Teresa, that this saintly woman, this
saint, literally, experienced profound
periods of midnight darkness created
by her sure conviction that God almighty, the Creator of Universe, and
Jesus, his son, had walked away and left
her completely alone – that they simply were not to be found. This woman,

Abraham Kuyper

doing his work, felt at times totally abandoned.

What do we do with that fact? How can we understand someone whose devotion to the Lord Jesus flags so fully? There were times in her life when half the world looked to her as the model of Christian living. By her own confession, she'd walked and talked with Jesus, listened to his very voice, heard his outline for how she and her Daughters of Charity should live. Who on earth could have been closer?

Yet, frequently, she felt alone in a darkness so complete that it seemed all-encompassing. She told few. How could she? After all, to millions she was the purest, shining light of the love of Jesus. "My own soul remains in deep darkness & desolation," she confessed to the archbishop (154).

Somewhere in *The Treasury of David*, Charles H. Spurgeon says that what Mother Teresa experienced is a form of darkness known only to believers, because only those who know the comfort of God's abiding love can feel the horror of being somehow bereft of his grace.

Whether we call it worry or anxiety or even depression – maybe even despair – it was, in her, very, very real, by her own admission and confession. Her biographers claim she used it – that horrific darkness – to more fully empathize with others. She guided her own personal suffering into the suffering of others, which, they say – and history may well prove – enabled her heart to grow, even as her spirit appeared to wither with the absence of her savior's voice.

Whether she prayed or read on those awful sleepless nights we'll never know, but if those who tell her story are right (and no one but Mother Teresa will ever know if they are) she used her own *despair* – and I don't use that word without regard – to understand the estrangement from God that others admitted. Thus, if we believe them, her biographers might say that she turned her own utter weakness into longsuffering strength.

But there will be more to say about the utter darkness that's here, almost unbelievably, in a book of private writings titled by her editor, thoughtfully, *Come Be My Light*.

PRAYER: Some of us, Lord, feel the darkness more profoundly and more often than others. Some of us find ourselves convinced that you've left the building, that you're nowhere to be found, that they've somehow wandered from the light of your presence. In those times especially, Lord, come be their light – and help those of us who don't feel that abandonment be whatever kind of beacon we can, to "be there" for those in great need. In the name of Jesus, Amen.

LI. Darkness (2)

You have put me in the lowest pit, in the darkest depths. Your wrath lies heavily on me; you have overwhelmed me with all your waves.

Psalm 88:6–7

It is abundantly clear from her own letter and notes that Mother Teresa – the most celebrated saint of her time, a woman who not long after her death was canonized by the Roman Catholic Church –suffered painfully from the darkness that descends on believers who feel banished from the presence of the Lord God. As to her doubt there is none. Often, in fact, "the bride of Christ" felt herself abandoned at the altar of life itself.

How on earth can such a humble, faithful servant of Christ be so adamant that his beloved presence has simply passed her by? How can someone who sacrificed her life to follow Jesus' own directions into the holes of the poor see before her all-encompassing darkness?

Thoughtful psychologists and psychiatrists may well have substantial, convincing theories, theories I'd love to hear by the way, because the conundrum will be, or so it seems to me, forever a mystery: how can someone so close to Christ feel him so irretrievably gone?

To me, there is no easy answer, save one. Simply stated, Mother Teresa, officially a saint, was human, and as such subject to the score of weaknesses our mutual flesh is heir to. She doubted because, often as not, all of us do. Think not? Read the psalms.

Some like to believe that her darkness was, in fact, a blessing. Here's the way Fr. Brian Kolodiejchuk, the editor of *Come Be My Light*, understands the burden of doubt that attended MT's life: "Interior darkness was Mother Teresa's privileged way of entering into the mystery of the Cross of Christ" (156).

It's a paradox, yet greatly understandable. I spoke to a man just last week who told me that his grandson's cancer was a horror, save one thing – the immense blessing of prayers and gifts of friends and strangers who helped his own daughter and her husband through the struggle. Once upon a time, a young woman told me that nothing in her life had changed her so fully, remade her into someone who had begun to care for others, as her cancer. Her boyfriend, a research chemist studying cancer itself, grimaced, I remember, as she said it because he didn't see those cancer cells as haloed as she did.

That suffering can be a blessing seems, to me, irrefutable. But we take the reality of suffering to another level when we see it as "a privileged way of entering into the mystery of the Cross of Christ."

If that's true, the utter spiritual darkness in which she found herself would have to be pure blessing – and it wasn't. She may well have had moments when she considered her estrangement from God to be exactly that; but if that was so, would suffering be suffering? If suffering is totally a blessing, then is it suffering at all? If it was, then why did she so clearly seek relief?

Fr. Kolodiejchuk would like it to be so, and he may well be right.

But there are moments when the Protestant that I am much prefers the empty cross to the crucifix, the risen Lord to the suffering Christ; and this is one of those moments. In my life at least, the despair that accompanies an across-the-board loss of hope has never been a better means by which to understand the mystery of Christ's suffering. It's always been a horrifying black hole.

To me, the wonderful good news of the gospel, here and always, is that even those we know as saints are human, not divine, subject to sin's own horrors; but, by way of grace alone, brought radiantly back into communion with the Lord, only by his hand.

Stuff happens in life, bad stuff. But he loves us, always. That's the real blessing.

PRAYER: Pass me not; O gentle Savior,
Hear my humble cry;
While on others Thou art calling,
Do not pass me by.

Trusting only in Thy merit,
Would I seek Thy face;
Heal my wounded, broken spirit,
Save me by Thy grace.

Savior, Savior,
Hear my humble cry,
While on others Thou art calling,
Do not pass me by. Amen.

(Frances J. Crossby)

LII. Darkness (3)

But I cry to you for help, LORD; in the morning my prayer comes before you. Why, LORD, do you reject me and hide your face from me? Psalm 88:13–14

Mother Teresa didn't tell the world about the darkness, but neither did she keep it a secret, scribbling out descriptions of her lonely days and nights outside the presence of God in some diary or journal. More than once – and to more than one person – she did more than simply hint at the painful emptiness in her heart and soul.

Her superior, Archbishop Périer, was the recipient of some of those notices, as in a letter in February, 1956. "I want to say to you something – but I do not know how to express it," she wrote at the outset of the letter. "I am longing – with a painful longing to be all for God – to be holy in such a way that Jesus can live His life to the full in me." And then this: "The more I want Him – the less I am wanted" (164).

Then again, in a letter to Jesuit Father Lawrence Trevor Picachy, who had led a spiritual retreat Mother Teresa had attended. After the retreat she told him that the two of them had much to appreciate in the spiritual vitality of her young colleagues, the ones he'd just met. But as for herself, "If you only knew what I am going through – He is destroying everything in me. – But as I hold no claim on myself – He is free to do anything. Pray for me that I keep smiling at Him" (169).

Or, once again to Father Périer, to whom she had to report on her work: "Pray for me – for within me everything is icy cold" (163).

There may be no clear answer to the question of how it could be that this woman, so dedicated, so pious, someone who considered herself a bride of Christ, could feel so fully shunned; but in one of those letters, Father Périer offered a possible answer by delving into yet another paradox of all of our lives – the odd pain some of us feel in the middle of what looks like success.

This "feeling of loneliness, of abandonment, of not being wanted," he told her, ". . . is willed by God in order to attach us to Him alone"; and it occurs, he said, as "an antidote to our external activities, . . . a way of keeping us humble in the midst of applauses, publicity, praises, appreciation, etc. and success." And then this: "To feel that we are nothing, that we can do nothing is the realisation of a fact" (167).

It is a fact that, far more quickly than anyone, including Mother Teresa, would have guessed, her new mission to the poor on the streets of Calcutta had prospered. Soon, it seemed, unforeseen gifts to the mission were accruing in abundance, even though her intent had been, from the outset, to minister to the poor as the poor. Young woman appeared as novitiates, and prayers were offered in all kinds, all over. "Applauses, publicity, praises, appreciation, etc.," flowed in, far beyond anything Mother Teresa had ever imagined.

Somehow, it's perfectly understandable that this little woman would have trouble accepting what most of the world might describe as *success*. After all, on the train to Darjeeling, Jesus had never mentioned anything about accolades, about praise and honor. What she wanted from the outset was not just the wardrobe of poverty but the soul of total penniless-ness. She wanted *not* to have food. She wanted to know the world as the poor knew it; she wanted to know the poor as the poor knew themselves.

What she never wanted and could never have imagined was celeb-rity.

She wanted only to serve.

The success of the mission could not have been the sole cause of Mother Teresa's darkness. Undoubtedly, there was more. Neurologists, today, may well think it was chemical – some drastic imbalance.

What we know, hard enough as it is to believe, is that this pervasive darkness, even in the life of a saint, was very, very real.

PRAYER: Come by our light, Lord, bring your radiance into every moment of our days and nights. Stay with us, live in our homes, abide on our streets, be our God, our Father, our hope and love. Amen.

LIII. Deception

May these words of my mouth and this meditation of my heart be pleasing in your sight, LORD, my Rock and my Redeemer. Psalm 19:14

I've often wondered why Nathaniel Hawthorne's *The Scarlet Letter* is as revered as it is, presumed by some to be the best American novel of the 19th century. For years, I used it in an intro class in American literature, and only rarely did it rouse students from mid-morning yawns.

Most don't really get it, don't understand why the preacher, Arthur Dimmesdale, for instance, would conceal his passion for Hester Prynne, lie about it in fact, and not claim his very own daughter, little Pearl. Love conquers all, right?

From Robert Vignola's 1934 film *The Scarlet Letter*

The implicit values of the novel simply don't jive with life today – a mid-19th century novel about mid-17th century Puritan New England. Besides, who really cares? What's more, the novel's complexity – Dimmesdale's complexity, Hester's complexity too – is its strength and genius. Readers who aren't interested in complexity find *The Scarlet Letter* an Everest simply not worth the fancy hiking shoes.

But it's Arthur Dimmesdale I think of when I read the letters, the confessions of a faithless Mother Teresa; Arthur Dimmesdale, whose own sermons had to taste like acid when he considered the deceitful fiction of his own life. Revered by his congregation and the entire community, he was, even as he accepted their praise, the most reverend of liars.

There's no scandal in Mother Teresa's life, at least none that anyone has ever uncovered. There's no illicit relationship, no graft or corruption, no crime, no drawer full of unmarked bills. What there is, however, is severe, sustained doubt, ten years' worth, darkness created by her perceived spiritual abandonment, by a God who was, for her at least, gone.

And in that time, not unlike Arthur Dimmesdale, Mother Teresa found herself in a position that required her to be a spiritual guide for many, in her case the leader of a dynamic, new sisterhood, the Missionaries of Charity, dedicated young women driven by the same passion Mother Teresa had used to inaugurate her ministry on the streets of Calcutta. Their leader, rapidly becoming a celebrity, found herself totally shut out from the eternal love of God – ". . . words pass through my [lips] and I long with a deep longing to believe in them," she once wrote (193).

I can't imagine the pain of having to say pious things, to bring consolation and strength, when she herself could find no similar path to oneness with God.

> The whole time smiling. – Sisters & people pass such remarks. – They think my faith, trust & love are filling my very being & that the intimacy with God and union to His will must be absorbing my heart. – Could they but know – and how my cheerfulness is the cloak by which I cover the emptiness & misery. (187)

Remarkably, and in a fashion that can only be characterized by one word – saintliness – she never seemingly doubted the love of God, even though she was convinced for years that she could not be a recipient of his favor.

"In my heart there is no faith – no love – no trust – there is so much pain – the pain of longing, the pain of not being wanted," she wrote to Jesus, a kind of assignment given her by Father Picachy. "I utter words of community prayers – and try my utmost to get out of every word the sweetness it has to give. – But my prayer of union is not there any longer. – I no longer pray." And yet, she wouldn't give up: "My soul is not one with You – and yet when alone in the streets – I talk to You for hours – of my longing for You" (193).

Unlike Arthur Dimmesdale, who is only a fiction, in every way, Mother Teresa, who is and was very real, is a testimony: by the gift of everything she had and was to those who lived "in the dark holes" of Calcutta's mean and dirty streets, to the pitiful darkness she suffered throughout those very times in her life when she was most revered, Mother Teresa is, in every human way, a model of abiding faith. She is a saint, even when she was convinced, absolutely, that she wasn't. Remarkable.

Doubt – severe, blanketing doubt – does not have to keep you or me or anyone we love from the throne of God. Mother Teresa was there, even when she didn't believe she was or ever could be.

Praise his holy name.

PRAYER: Dear sovereign Lord, bless us always with faith, even when it seems so much an allusion. Thank you for the gift of Mother Teresa, who taught us how to love others, even when they are unlovable; and to love ourselves, even when we feel ourselves so greatly unworthy. Stay close to us, Lord, our rock and our redeemer. Amen.

LIV. OUR FEARS AND HERS

Make every effort to live in peace with everyone and to be holy; without holiness no one will see the Lord. Hebrews 12:14

We had again trouble at Kalighat [Nirmal Hriday] – they very coolly told me I must thank God that up to now I have not received a shot or a beating from them, since all those who worked for them death has been their reward. Very peacefully I told them, that I was ready to die for God. Hard times are coming, let us pray that our Society will stand the test of Charity. (152)

I'm not altogether sure what Mother Teresa considered to be "the test of Charity," but one can infer from what she says in this note to Archbishop Périer, that it was something a good deal more than keeping pantry shelves full of food or pots and pans sparkling. She implies that for her as well as the needy, physical danger, even death was lurking in "the holes of the poor," and that assessing the Society's successes could prove difficult if one of the Missionaries of Charity were actually to die carrying out the mission.

Calcutta's slums in the post-war period go far beyond anything some North American might imagine. Comparing people's relative suffering is always impossible, and yet it's fair to say that even the most impoverished children in these United States will not likely be turned down for medical care if they're carried, as they often are, to Emergency.

Not so in Calcutta. People died on the streets, their bodies left to rot. The poor of Calcutta lived in impoverishment unlike anything most of us can imagine – and that level of poverty often breeds violence. What the Missionaries of Charity did on the streets was often dangerous work.

Consider also the depth of darkness Mother Teresa faced for a very long time, a darkness she really had to cover in order to lead the young women who came to work with her. Imagine for a moment how hard it must have been to wear a smile, to give comfort, to cheer the depressed when she felt herself totally alone in the world, abandoned somehow by the God she meant to serve with every bit of her being, every moment of her life.

What I'm saying is that it's not hard to build a case for a daily life lived in torturous difficulty, torment, and fear. I am confident that her prayers were unceasing, that she asked every day to be freed from the problems she faced all around, from dangers within and violence without.

It's impossible for me to go on right now without smiling, for, by her own confession, what shook her world unmercifully, what scared her half to death, was not the war without or the battles within, but – stay with me here – speaking to large crowds. The Missionaries of Charity grew in reach and reputation; and in the fall of 1960, for the first time since she'd come to Calcutta in 1929, she left India, bound for the United States, for Las Vegas – of all places! – where she'd been asked to speak at a convention of the National Council of Catholic Women.

Was she stretching it a bit when she said, "My going to U.S. – was the hardest act of obedience I had ever had to give to God" (204)? Was speaking to 3000 women more difficult than answering the call to mission, than walking the desolate streets around her, than facing the darkness within? Seems impossible.

But human. But incredibly and authentically human. She was scared to death of a microphone.

To know the story is to understand the humanness of this tiny woman. She was a saint, not because there was something about her that made her greater than others, but because she listened to the Lord and did extraordinary things in his name out of obedience. She was not an angel and in no way divine.

But she did saintly things, as all of us know – all of us believers. She modeled courage and love in a way few have done.

But put her in front of a microphone and she wilted.

Mother Teresa was a composite of flesh and blood and soul. She was only one of us, just another of God's own children.

PRAYER: Thank you for the life of Mother Teresa, Lord – thank you for blessing us with what she did in her obedience to your will, your command to love. Strengthen our resolve to live "in you," as she worked so hard to do. Amen.

LV. THE FORTUNATE FALL

For it is by grace you have been saved, through faith – and this is not from yourselves, it is the gift of God. . . . Ephesians 2:8

One of the most famous yarns about Martin Luther, who was, among other things, a marvelously colorful character, is the story of him as a young monk, on his knees, climbing the stairs in front of a building called the Lateran Palace when he was, for the very first time, in Rome, the heart of religious life during Luther's time.

Through the years that have passed since the earliest decades of the 16th century, the story now comes to us in several versions; but what each emphasizes is the suffering Luther pushed himself into, on those 28 stone stairs, as he attempted, on his knees, to send someone romping joyfully out of purgatory and into heaven.

What's true and what's myth will never be known, but dispute is silly on one point: what Luther learned and eventually taught is that salvation arrived in our lives not by indulgence, or bloody penance or bloody knees, or even an entire lifetime of "Hail Marys," but by grace alone, a gift of God. Grace isn't win-able, even by profound suffering. We can't pay the price for sin, only Jesus can. Grace is the loving gift of a loving God. Nobody earns it. No way. No how.

Martin Luther

Before Luther stumbled on the Bible's own definition of grace, before he discovered that no sentence of stony stairs can atone for sin, young Martin was sorely troubled, at times to the point of death itself. His profound doubts, like Mother Teresa's, were legion and prompted similarly dark despair.

In *Luther*, Eric Till's 2003 film, one of young Martin's superiors in the monastery asks him if he'd ever read the New Testament. When Martin says no, the superior says he will, now that he's off to Wittenberg. Luther is shocked. "Here I am losing my faith, feeling like a fool, even to pray, and you're sending me away?" he asks.

"You'll preach," the superior says.

When Luther says he'll be a fraud as a preacher, the Superior tells him, "We preach best what we need to learn most."

It's always been a fascinating kind of psychological paradox to me – that preachers (and, okay, writers too) do their very best at what they need to learn. Nathaniel Hawthorne's Puritan prelates are always better preachers when they've got something to hide – take the good Rev. Hooper from "The Minister's Black Veil," for instance. Especially in my tradition, in which the preacher was once addressed only as "dominie," the possibility of the preacher being anything less than a paragon of personal virtue is almost scandalous.

With good reason. It seems to me that had Mother Teresa ever confessed the grave depth of her own doubt to those who served with her on the streets, such a revelation of the profoundest doubt certainly could have made her sisters doubt the ministry. So she held back her honesty, which probably may have made her doubt worse and certainly more excruciating.

"The place of God in my soul is blank. – There is no God in me," she wrote to a superior, Father Joseph Neuner, when he asked her to write out her inner trials. "When the pain of longing is so great – I just long & long for God – and then it is that I feel – He does not want me – He is not there" (210).

And then, remarkably, she says this: "My heart & soul & body belongs only to God – that He has thrown away as unwanted the child of His Love. – And to this, Father, I have made that resolution in this retreat – To be at his disposal" (212).

I don't know that anyone can or will ever determine how it was that a woman with such massive faith could have become so spiritually penniless – could have, for years by her own admission, no faith at all. But what seems to be true is that her own deprivation – God's own absence in her own life, her prayer life, her devotional life – only strengthened her resolve in the life of service and love that she carried out on the dark streets of Calcutta.

Only in the poor did she see Jesus.

Understanding grace made a great difference in the life of Martin Luther. Sometimes I can't help but wonder whether Mother Teresa, saint though she is, could have been lifted from her near despondency by a reminder that our owning salvation is not something that comes by a purchase any of us could have made.

But she knew. She had to know. She just had to. She just couldn't believe it somehow, and she's likely not alone.

PRAYER: May the peace of Christ be ours this day, Lord. May your Son's glorious self come into our lives as palpably as the land we walk, the air we breathe, the sun we see before us. Chase our doubts with the sweep of your Holy Spirit. Thank you for life eternal. Thank you for grace itself. Amen.

LVI. Fort and Rez

So Christ himself gave the apostles, the prophets, the evangelists, the
pastors and teachers, to equip his people for works of service, so that
the body of Christ may be built up until we all reach unity in the
faith and in the knowledge of the Son of God and become mature,
attaining to the whole measure of the fullness of Christ. Ephesians
4:11–13

So this old friend of mine and his good wife decided to leave the reservation, where, as a teacher, he'd lived happily for decades. They decided
to depart the Southwest for the Northwest, the place they'd both grown
up, the place he said the two of them would always call "home." When
they told their Native friends they were leaving the rez, my old friends
explained the move this way: "we're going back to our own reservation."
His Native friends, he said, understood totally.

I've lived on *my* reservation for almost all of my own threescore
and five years. This Dutch Calvinist has lived among Dutch Calvinists –
sometimes peaceably, sometimes not – for his entire professional life and
more. One could argue – and some do – that our most bitter fights are
those we carry on with those we love, with family; but I don't think I'm
overstating when I say that my life has been lived within the walls of a
fort where life has been, at least for me, most familiar, if not accommo-
dating, as a pocketful of peppermints.

Another friend, someone who's never lived on her own reservation
but always on others', once explained to me why she'd chosen to live the
way she has, consistently among the world's poor and misbegotten. I
don't remember her words exactly, but the gist of them went something
like this: I know myself, and I know that if I weren't engaged somewhere,
well, dangerous, I honestly wouldn't be safe – not from others, but from
myself.

I translated that explanation in this way: my faith in God flourishes
bountifully only on dirty streets and in woebegone hovels, places where
it's tough to believe.

Perhaps some fine psychiatrist could explain the darkness in the life,
in the heart and soul of Mother Teresa, but I'm powerless. All I can do

is sit in astonishment at how a woman so devoted to listening to Jesus could actually spend years never, ever hearing his voice. How could a woman who begged Christ to come and be her light, live so desperately in midnight?

Father Kolodiejchuk tries to explain it this way: ". . . it was only when she was with the poor that she perceived His presence vividly. There she felt Him to be so alive and so real" (212–213).

I think I could create a rack on which to torture myself when I stoop in the shadow of an assessment like that, for I haven't lived among the poor, the homeless, the voiceless. I've been, after all, a professor, touting the importance of literature and writing. What I've witnessed of the degradation of poverty has appeared only from the ink on a page or photograph. Strictly speaking, I haven't fed the poor, clothed the homeless, visited prisoners, or picked my starving neighbor from the ditch. I've lived my life in a fortress.

But then, even scripture says not everyone is called to Calcutta. Some are teachers and preachers and milkers and pastry chefs. Some ride horses and others ride juries. Some practice law, others the oboe. Some sell used cars. Some raid meth kitchens. Some raise kids and some raise heck. Some live on mountaintops, others rarely leave the kitchen.

Just about the only law we all live with is the one about obedience. Those of us who confess the name of Jesus, give it our best on whatever acre of ground we're called to, whether it's inside the fortress or some scruffy place off the reservation.

Obedience is what the Christian life is all about, but it's much easier to say than it is to do. Good Lord, help us all.

PRAYER: In whatever it is we do, wherever it is we go, give us the wherewithal to follow your guiding hand, strengthen us in all things and in obedience to your will and your word, Lord. Help us live faithfully in the fortress of your love. Amen.

LVII. Eucharist

And he took bread, gave thanks and broke it, and gave it to them, saying, "This is my body. . . ." Luke 22:19

Somewhere along the line – maybe middle school – I learned something about the words *transubstantiation* and *consubstantiation*, maybe the biggest words I knew back then, other than *supercalifragilisticexpialidocious*. I remember those words because I remember the concept – well, sort of. One of the words described the Roman Catholic view of the Lord's Supper, another Lutheran, and yet another word, one I've forgotten, was ours, the Reformed view of the sacrament.

That I know the words means I found the whole discussion quite interesting some time way back when. What I'm saying is I was familiar with the arguments in a classroom sense, but I really didn't understand them or own them until I met Kevin Conroy, high school principal at the high school where I spent my first two years as a teacher, forty years ago.

Kevin Conroy had a thick Brooklyn accent, having grown up in "New Yawk," grown up devout Irish Catholic, emphasis on *devout*. I don't know that other teachers knew him back then as I did, but he was my first boss and I was totally single, living like a monk in abject devotion to school, and often – it's true – painfully lonely. All those things he seemed to understand.

Mr. Conroy and I shared something rich and, for me at least, bountiful. We were both serious believers – he was more devout, but we were both serious. I didn't go to church much back then, but the Calvinism in my system didn't dissipate. So the two of us would talk – about faith, about religion, about God.

One after-school afternoon, we talked about communion, an event he called "the Eucharist." It may well have been the first time in my life that I put to use the old classroom terminology, the first time I learned something real about communion, not as a concept but as a significant life event.

"Jim," he told me, every bit of his Irish soul flaring in intensity, "when I take the host into my mouth, it is no symbol – it *is* Jesus Christ."

He wasn't creating an argument; what he said had the heartfelt abundance of raw and real testimony– he was witnessing, in the very best sense of that word. Somehow, my soul's memory found a place for that moment, and I never forgot it. In an abstract sense, that day he made a convert of this Calvinist.

Kevin Conroy gave me the means by which to understand how it was that Mother Teresa, who for so many years had to slug through spiritual despondency, simply could not and would not miss Holy Communion, even though Jesus, indeed God almighty, had seemingly left her out in the cold. Even when she claimed he'd forgotten her, she held stubbornly to the faith that animated Kevin Conroy's own testimony – because she believed, heart and soul, that when she participated in the Eucharist, she was eating God's own precious body and blood.

"This is my body," Christ said. To Kevin Conroy and Mother Teresa and millions of other Roman Catholics, it is. It's just that simple.

Eugene Peterson once told me that he doesn't bother explaining that the bread and wine are merely symbols because he knows the institution of the Lord's Supper is vastly richer when we don't consider that what we're doing is something akin to shadow boxing. At a certain level, insisting on the character of Reformation theology only cheapens the sacrament. Thanks, in great part, to my old school principal, I couldn't agree more.

"Her adoring attitude," a senior sister once wrote of Mother Teresa, "gestures such as genuflections – even on both knees, in the presence of the Blessed Sacrament exposed, and that well into old age – her postures such as kneeling and joining hands, her preference for receiving Holy Communion on the tongue all bespoke her faith in the Eucharist" (213).

I don't doubt for a moment that some of us Protestants would demur from that assessment, or the theology underlying it. But Kevin Conroy taught me long ago that "her faith in the Eucharist" really means her faith in Jesus Christ.

The image of her there, taking Christ, even in her own travail, on her knees, penitent, receiving the host, is as beautiful a portrait as this Calvinist can imagine.

PRAYER: Fill us with your grace, Lord, bring us into your presence with your word, your spirit, and the sacraments you gave us so lovingly. Amen.

LVIII. "Bewonderment"

Be exalted, O God, above the heavens; let your glory be over all the earth. Psalm 57:11

The basic paradigm by which I've always seen the Christian life is the outline of a drama that rises from the handbook of doctrine with which I was raised. That outline goes like this: "sin, salvation, service."

The story line begins with sin – our knowledge of it, as it exists within us. Calvin starts even a bit earlier, with the heavens, with our sense of God as manifest in his world: what we see and experience. Because humans can't help but see God's marvelous work in the heavens and the earth around us, we come to know that there *is* a God. With that knowledge, we feel our own limitations – that we *aren't* God. And there begins our knowledge of human limits, our knowledge, finally, of sin.

That conviction draws us closer to God because we need a Savior. Sin precedes salvation, or so the story goes, through the second act.

Once we know that he loves us in spite of our sin, our hearts fill, our souls rejoice; we can't help but celebrate our salvation. That celebration leads us into gratitude and service, into doing what we can to be his agents of love in the world he loves so greatly.

Sin, salvation, service – three acts of a drama that is the plot of all of our lives.

Mother Teresa's take on a very similar tale in three different acts was created, I suppose, by her experiences in the ghettos of Calcutta. We begin with repulsion: what we see, she says – brokenness, sadness – offends, prompts us to look away.

But we really can't or shouldn't or won't; we have to look misery in its starving face, and when we do, we move from repulsion to compassion – away from rejection and toward loving acceptance. End Act II.

The final act is what she called "bewonderment," which is sheer wonder plus a-grade admiration. Our compassion leads us to bewonderment.

"Bewonderment" is likely one of those words no one uses but everyone understands. Still, like *reverence*, it's hard to come by in a world where our sorest needs are never more than a price tag away.

I'll admit that *bewonderment* is hard to come by for me, perhaps because it isn't so clearly one of the chapters in the story I was told as a boy, the story that is still deeply embedded in my soul. "Service" is the end of the Christian life – or always has been – for me, not "bewonderment."

I'm more than a little envious of David's praise in Psalm 57. What he says to God in prayer is something I rarely tell him. I don't think I've ever asked God *not* to hide his little light under a bushel, to display his radiant grace from pole-to-pole in my life and yours. I'm forever asking for favors, some big, some not, but am only rarely into adoration, in part, I suppose, because I'm so rarely in awe.

But bewonderment, awe, is something I'm learning, even this morning, and for that I'm thankful – for the book of songs, for David, and for the God David knew so intimately that he could speak the way he does in Psalm 57.

It's difficult for some of us to be intimate with God – to be so close to a being so great and grand and seemingly out of reach. But bewonderment is something I think we can learn, all of us, even an old man, if we learn to see.

PRAYER: Thank you for lessons learned, even if school is almost a lifetime behind us. Thank you for allowing us to be thrilled, to be surprised, to be excited, to feel bewonderment – and thank you for all the Mother Teresas who teach us how to see. Amen.

LIX. A Blessing from the Rosary

May these words of my mouth and this meditation of my heart be pleasing in your sight, LORD, my Rock and my Redeemer. Psalm 19:14

The other day I can't tell you how bad I felt. – There was a moment when I nearly refused to accept. – Deliberately I took the Rosary and very slowly without even meditating or thinking – I said it slowly and calmly. The moment passed. . . . (238, Letter to Bishop Picachy)

I was 32 years old when someone at Bread Loaf Writers' Conference called to tell me that my application for a scholarship had been accepted and they were offering me a position as a waiter. I had no idea what that meant, but I understood proudly that the offer was a good, good thing.

It's now more another 32 years later, but I will never forget receiving that call because I felt that my being chosen for a scholarship to the granddaddy of all writers conferences, Bread Loaf, signaled fame and fortune.

When I flew into Burlington, Vermont, for the conference, I met another conferee, a woman my age, married with two children, an aspiring poet. Ten days later, when we boarded a plane to leave, she and I stood on the stairway to a small jet, waiting to enter the cabin. She looked at me and shook her head. "I hope this plane crashes," she told me.

The atmosphere during that mountaintop retreat had been electric. Aspiring writers like me flirted daily with National Book Award winners, editors, agents, and publishers. Life – dawn 'till dawn – was always on stage. She'd been wooed by a celebrity poet, and she'd fallen in every way. Now, regrettably, she had to go back to real life.

I'll admit it – I wasn't accustomed to either the pace or the character of life at Bread Loaf.

On a Sunday morning, I had walked away from people to a green Adirondack chair in a broad meadow, where I sat for an hour, thinking simply about my little son's soft arm, trying to imagine what it would feel like in my fingers, all the while reciting the familiar words of the 23rd psalm.

That moment is likely the closest I ever came to meditation, and I'll never forget it.

When the Rosary was recited over the radio when I was a boy, my parents raised an eyebrow, rolled their eyes, and turned it off – "vain repetition," we were always told, quoting the gospel's admonition against such tomfoolery. I never thought of the Rosary as anything else.

But when I think of Mother Teresa's besieged soul, when I see her sitting in silence, her fingers on each separate bead while repeating those prayers over and over again, I don't think of all those repetitions as being in any way, shape, or form vain.

When our ritual is empty, it isn't ritual at all. But when it's earnest as it was at least one day in the life of Mother Teresa, when it's undertaken in passionate desire for peace and joy, then it is, in a way even a Calvinist might acknowledge, sacramental.

That green Adirondack chair sits in a defined place in my soul's memory, I swear. As does Mother Teresa, stooping, praying, meditating, beads in hand, in an impassioned ritual I may likely never share, in nearly faithless hope of a spiritual blessing, even if only for a day, peace to quell the heavy burden of her doubt.

PRAYER: Fill our rituals with meaning, Lord. Help us to participate in our own exercises of faith with willing and loving hearts, anticipating that by prayer and supplication we can and will be blessed. Amen.

Adirondack chairs, Bread Loaf, Vermont

LX. SELFLESSNESS

For it is by grace you have been saved, through faith – and this is not from yourselves, it is the gift of God. . . . Ephesians 2:8

I was neither crushed nor heartbroken. It hadn't worked out, this long-distance relationship she thought essential in defining our relationship. You'll go to one college, and I'll go to another, she'd explained when we were in our last year of high school. It was the kind of test she wanted – if *we* could last through a 500-mile separation, then viola! – we'd be a real thing, maybe even marry, although at 19 we were a long way from that kind of talk.

We failed, although it's fair to say that she was the one who turned away. I was the faithful one – I kept *troth*, a word I'm sure I didn't know back then, but makes me sound severely saintly. She didn't, and, come summer, she broke it off, whatever *it* was we had, as they say. This isn't spin.

Anyway, my grandma held down a seat on a bench full of neighborhood widows who, over coffee, likely held court on a variety of characters and issues, including, obviously, her grandson and his love life. She was trying to be sweet, I'm sure, when she told me what she did once the relationship was history. "Well, you know what the ladies say," she told me, lovingly, "– maybe it's better it's over because she would have been the one who wore the pants."

Makes me giggle yet today, 44 years later.

And I can't help thinking about what she said with respect – strangely enough! – to Mother Teresa because what she wanted more than anything, it seems, is to be abjectly selfless, not to wear the pants, ever. She wanted to be nothing for her Lord. She wanted him to be her's. "I want to be at his disposal," she wrote, often. *Disposal,* she said. I want to be rid of me.

I don't have any doubt that the reason my grandmother's double-edged comfort stays with me is because the image she created isn't necessarily sympathetic of her grandson – Mickey Milquetoast, a pushover, a patsy.

But then, in any relationship – even a marriage – selflessness is a virtue, right? – the polar opposite of pride, the first of the seven deadlies. But I didn't read the implication of grandma's assessment as positive. I didn't want to be spineless. Who does?

That Jesus Christ wants us to live for him goes without saying. That he wants us, all of us, every bit of us, is a doctrine of scripture that no one can deny – heart, soul, and strength. That Mother Teresa would want to be selfless in the divine presence of her Savior is not only understandable but saintly. "All to thee, my blessed Savior – I surrender all."

Few believers in the history of the 20th century have come to epitomize so clearly true Christian service as Mother Teresa. Few believers could – and yet fewer believers have – so devoutly wished to be "disposed" of by Jesus Christ.

But the hard-core Calvinist in me can't help but wonder if her life-long passion to be at "the disposal" of her Lord didn't create something inverse, a rich and revealing self-abnegation that, psychologically speaking, made her feel totally unworthy of the very attention and love she so passionately craved. Her fervent desire to be nothing left her, oddly enough, somehow believing that she was far beyond the reach of his love.

Is there a limit to selflessness? What God wants, as orthodoxy would have it, is the death of "the old man of sin," but not our death, nor our disposal. Does ardent selflessness somehow require the doubt, the darkness that Mother Teresa lived with for so many years?

That her suffering brought her closer to the suffering Christ is understandable, but we do – don't we? – worship a risen Lord. Mother Teresa's life is the very model of love, of Christian charity, of service devoutly to be praised. She is, even in this Calvinist's sense, a saint.

But that her despair in his absence needs to be understood as necessary to her saintliness on the streets of Calcutta seems somehow wrong.

Even in the royal robes of her righteousness, or so it seems to me, this saint remains one of us, a human being and, as such, just as all of us are, in need of grace.

On that score, I think she wouldn't demur.

PRAYER: Lord, we stand in need of your grace, your forgiveness, your love – all of us. We thank you for your atonement, our glory, the life you so freely give us in your resurrection. Amen.

LXI. A Terrible Longing

Do not be anxious about anything, but in every situation, by prayer and petition, with thanksgiving, present your requests to God. And the peace of God, which transcends all understanding, will guard your hearts and your minds in Christ Jesus. Philippians 4:6–7

Reading Jamie Quatro puts a reader like me in an extremely unfamiliar place, smack dab in the middle of the torture a woman, a young woman, knows when she determines that her affair with a man other than her husband cannot – simply cannot – continue. Despite her absolute certainty, her heartfelt conviction that it must end, his sudden absence from her life is a loss as traumatic as death itself – or so Ms. Quatro claims. Figuratively, in that woman's mind, her heart, and in her body, the other man must die to save her marriage.

One of the highly imaginative stories from Ms. Quatro's first collection, *I Want to Show You More*, starkly places that "other man," dead, his body decomposing, in the adulteress's own marriage bed, her husband beside them both. It's a striking image, a mark of her creative strengths as a writer.

What animates the story is the narrator's "terrible longing," *terrible* meaning something so awful it's painful. And yet, what she feels is longing. The phrase is an oxymoron, two mutually contradictory terms juxtaposed as if they're not mutually contradictory. Some oxymorons get used so often that they've morphed into cliché: sweet sorrow and living dead. But all of them are rooted in paradox, and paradox – or so it seems to me – lies forever at the heart of human experience in part because it's so undeniably human to, for instance, want what we don't want.

The torture that results from such inhuman humanness is the stuff of story, even of legend. Listen to Romeo:

"O heavy lightness! serious vanity!
Mis-shapen chaos of well-seeming forms!
Feather of lead, bright smoke, cold fire, sick health!"

Words go to war in an oxymoron, a madness that still somehow makes sense.

And, self-confessedly, it's at the heart of Mother Teresa's darkness.

Accolades were arising from around the world, her sisterhood was being lauded for its selflessness, the poor on the streets of Calcutta were being loved, daily, but the longing that lay deepest within the heart and soul of Mother Teresa was, for years, unmet.

"My feelings are so treacherous," she wrote to her bishop, "I feel like 'refusing God' and yet, the biggest and the hardest to bear – is this terrible longing for God" (245).

She had no way of understanding the darkness she found in her own soul, a darkness created by Jesus' own absence; and the result was a "terrible longing," all-consuming need, passion unsatisfied. What she wanted so badly, she seemed incapable of receiving – the love of Jesus, his words, his comfort. Her love was unrequited. In her heart, Jesus Christ had walked away from his bride, sentencing her to years of this torture, this terrible longing.

Confessions like this were so few and so limited – only to her superiors, and then only to some – that it's helpful to remember that not once did this Sister of Charity stop working, not once did she falter in what she gave to the poor, not once did her witness on the killing streets of Calcutta flounder. She well may have felt Christ's absence in her soul, but she never faltered in carrying out what, long ago, Christ had demanded of her.

She may have had "treacherous" feelings, may have had days, even weeks, when she considered simply "refusing God"; but she never did, even though, by our standards, she almost certainly had cause.

Mother Teresa is, via the exacting standards of the Roman Catholic Church, a saint. She gave her life in dedication to the plight of the poor in ghettos of unimaginable suffering. She deliberately chose to live with the poor amid their poverty and even squalor. She took on their suffering, and hers is a life of shining witness.

But when we consider this terrible longing of hers for a lover she believed, with all her heart, had left her, and when we remember that her devotion to God almighty and the least of these his children never flagged, then there is another reason to celebrate this mighty little woman – pure and simple, the enormity of her faith.

PRAYER: Grant us the longing that Mother Teresa had to do your work in the world, Lord. Grant us the patience to wait upon your will. Grant us the peace that rises from your verifiable presence in our lives. Grant us the faith to know you are there. And then, after all that granting, God, turn us out into your world to spread the glory of your love. Amen.

LXII. To Be Alone

How long, LORD? Will you forget me forever? How long will you hide your face from me? How long must I wrestle with my thoughts and day after day have sorrow in my heart? Psalm 13:1–2

More gun deaths result from suicide than murder. Seriously. More Americans take their own lives than the number who die from car accidents. Seems impossible.

Never in my life have I read the local obituaries as closely as I do now that I'm getting old; still, the facts I just mentioned shock me. But then, I'm sure that very few obits would ever mention suicide; few, in fact, divulge cause of death.

Maybe I'm shocked because I'm not a coroner. Perhaps people don't tell the truth aloud, especially in a small town like the one I call home. Still, more suicides than murders?

I just finished teaching *Hamlet* again, and Act V's graveyard scene always has to be explained to kids – college or high school: Claudius and Gertrude cut a deal with the church, a deal that allowed Ophelia's body to buried somewhat honorably, despite her having taken her own life. However, the priest had insisted that not all of the rites ordinarily given to someone of her class and standing could be granted to her body, given the means of death. Her brother, Laertes, is incensed when he sees her dishonored by such paltry rites. He jumps in the grave, Hamlet goes in after him – and we've got action.

Kids today have trouble believing that not all that long ago the mortal coil of those who took their own lives would be buried somewhere less honorable than the community cemetery. People reasoned that suicide grew from despair so desperate that there could have been no hope, and the hopeless, ultimately, are faithless. Thus, no "Christian" burial.

Compared with life a century ago, we're dashingly more affluent. The poor we have with us always, but comparing our lives with much of the developing world, we're loaded. Despite our wealth, people kill themselves at alarming rates.

Loneliness, people say, creates a level of sad resignation that can all too easily lead to suicide. A life without human intimacy is a life that is alone. Some say, as a society, as a culture, we prize our own freedoms so greatly that we've begun to eschew traditional institutions like family, church, work, and play. If we bowl at all, we bowl alone. We hole up in our own worlds, some of them virtual, then feel stranded on the island we've created, where the commodity we most need – the loving touch of another human being – is impossible.

But tragedy is rarely that simply diagnosed. Few human beings were more celebrated than Mother Teresa, few touched more lives, few were more universally loved. Literally – physically – she touched thousands who loved her. Yet, her own terrifying isolation, hard as it is to believe, brought immense psychic and emotional pain: "nothing enters my soul," she told a friend, a priest, someone she'd wanted to speak to, but simply couldn't. "I was longing to speak to you in Bombay – yet I did not even try to make it possible." And then this: "If there is hell – this must be one" (250).

Who knows? It's possible to argue that few human beings gave away more love in the 20th century than Mother Teresa; yet her own isolation seemed unrelenting.

To know that about her makes us all sad. But to those who know the depths of loneliness and darkness that she suffered something of what they do is oddly comforting. We are not alone. We are never alone.

PRAYER: "Dwell in me, O blessed Spirit!
How I need Thy help divine!
In the way of life eternal,
Keep, O keep this heart of mine!"
In every way, Lord, in the way of this life and the next, keep our hearts safe in the intimate comfort and love of your "help divine."
Amen.

LXIII. AMAZING GRACE

For it is by grace you have been saved, through faith – and this is not from yourselves, it is the gift of God – not by works, so that no one can boast. Ephesians 2:8–9

It had to have been a troublesome question – "have you never had any doubt about God?" That's what he asked her, a journalist, someone undoubtedly given to announce her answer as publically as a billboard, maybe more so. He was writing her story, after all.

Anyone who reads her letters and notes knows the answer, sort of. Of her doubts, there were many: doubts the size and intensity of a killer twister, doubts that Jesus loved her, doubts that she was worthy, doubts that her savior was anywhere near Calcutta.

But that's not the way she answered the writer's question. "There was no doubt," she told the journalist. ". . . The moment you accept, the moment you surrender yourself, that's the conviction" (259).

Excuse me?

Did MT lie? I don't think so. Mother Teresa's doubt had far more to do with her than it did with Jesus, far less to do with his love than her unworthiness to receive it. It's impossible not to think her answer wasn't heartfelt truth – "There was no doubt," she told him, and she meant it, no matter what we might think ourselves.

And let's be clear here. I'm not sure anyone – even Mother Teresa – really understands grace. An old preacher once told me he thought it more than passing strange that we human beings love to get most anything we can for free . . . except grace, which all of us really want to earn. Most every Christian I know wants to be worthy of God's love, to be someone God smiles upon because, my goodness, we've battled the tempter for all these years and kept him at bay. We've run a good race. We've kept the faith. We've deliberately walked the paths of righteousness.

To all of that, grace says, "Big deal."

I can't help but think once again of Martin Luther climbing the Scale Santa, going up the stairs in Rome in the prescribed way, the holy way, on his knees, only to get to the top and be haunted by the conviction of a false promise. The story goes that once on the top stair, his mind kept saying, the just shall live by faith, not works – that any man should boast. That's the way the story goes.

"Without Him I can do nothing," Mother Teresa told the reporter. "But even God could do nothing for someone already full." And then: "You have to be completely empty to let Him in to do what He will" (260).

Completely empty, she told him. Completely, totally empty.

I'm not sure any human being in her time did as much to empty herself as did Mother Teresa. She'd promised her body and soul, in life and in death, to her faithful savior Jesus Christ; she tried to be nothing, nothing at all. Still, she spent most of her life determined that he'd somehow abandoned her.

Maybe what she wanted to feel was her own unworthiness, what she wanted to offer God himself was a life that had absolutely nothing to do with self, a life that was not her life but his. She attempted self-abasement to be loved by the God who'd sent her on a mission she'd begun and then run among the poorest of the poor. Because she needed to be nothing, she got down on her knees and suffered the debasement of selflessness because she wanted so badly to love and be loved.

I don't know that anyone really understands grace, understands love that is totally unmerited, catches on to the logic of the gift of life forever. Like the Galatians, for some human reason, we all want to earn it.

All of us.

PRAYER: You are so far beyond us, our perceptions, our senses, even our imagination, Lord. We thank you for your son, who helps us, fallen as we are, to see you, the Father. But we know too that your grace alone accounts for our life in you, your gift, your love. Amen.

LXIV. BE THE ONE

And being in anguish, he prayed more earnestly, and his sweat was like drops of blood falling to the ground. When he rose from prayer and went back to the disciples, he found them asleep, exhausted from sorrow. Luke 22:44–45

The American Puritans exercised a kind of typology that may well have been, finally, their own undoing. Their strict attention to the very words of scripture suggested parallels that were, I'm sure, as exciting to them as they were perilous. In the pattern of a persecuted people, they left England as if they were Israelites bound for the promised land. Their reading of the story of God's chosen people opened its arms to them in a fashion that allowed them to identify with the people of Israel so completely that the distinction between biblical history and their own was gone.

The horror of such close identification – and there are horrors – is that those who read themselves into the Bible's story can all too easily identify those forces working against them as the cavalry of the Great Deceiver. We are God's chosen – if you're against us, you're against him. Dissent becomes deviltry.

Maybe that's why I've always been skeptical of the kind of identification that too quickly makes claims for who gets the love of God – and who gets his scorn and punishment. It's not difficult for a steadfast believer to identify too closely with the great biblical stories.

But then, it may be I read the Bible too historically, to at-a-distance. One can err, I'm sure, in both extremes. Mother Teresa, for instance, had no similar problem. Her strengths sometimes arose from her immediate identification with the gospel stories she so treasured.

There's another t-shirt-quality phrase in her lexicon that I should really try to market. It has all kinds of possibilities, and it's built on her intimate identification with a gospel account that itself is unforgettable.

The night Jesus' passion begins, he takes some of his closest friends along to the Mount of Olives to pray, to ponder the events he knows all too well are coming. It's going to be an all-nighter, hours of bloody sweat-filled supplication to his own blessed Father.

And when, just for a moment, he turns away, he looks around only to see his friends, his disciples, his hand-picked, lovingly-nurtured followers, fast asleep. What a bunch of dunderheads. Their thoughtlessness in the inky darkness is unimaginable. But we weren't there.

"Be with Jesus," Mother Teresa used to tell her sisters. "He prayed and prayed, and then He went to look for consolation, but there was none." And then she'd say this: "I always write that sentence, 'I looked for one to comfort Me, but I found no one'" (260).

And then she'd write, she said, "Be the one."

Be the one.

Really, let's make that t-shirt cardinal red, bright red, signifying that bloody sweat, and then let's paste those three fat words in fat, white stripes across the front in a pattern that plasters the chest. Nothing fine or fancy. No old-fashioned calligraphy or some scripted nonsense – I want "Be the one" as pushy as a sandwich board.

Be the one.

Be the one.

I never read the late-night story just like that, never thought of it, really. I was too taken by those disciples nodding off as if the Mount of Olives was a dim-lit, all-night train station.

Be the one. Big, bold letters. It ought to be written on my heart.

PRAYER: Help us each to be the one, Lord, the one who will do your work, who will heal the sick, help the blind to see, cheer the faint of heart, love the unlovable. Grant us strength and commitment to be the one. Amen.

LXV. Providence and Planning

. . . establish the work of our hands for us – yes, establish the work of our hands. Psalm 90:17

In 1994, Dr. Robin Fox, editor of *The Lancet*, a leading journal for medical professionals, toured Mother Teresa's mission in Calcutta to have a look at the nature of care given the needy. The report he created is thought of today as being largely sympathetic.

Some criticism, he determined, was in order, however. There were moments and events he observed, he said, when some additional diagnostic testing was called for and available but simply not undertaken. "Such systematic approaches are alien to the ethos of the home," he wrote.

And then this line: "Mother Teresa prefers providence to planning. . ." What he means, of course, is that he observed events when, in his opinion, more scientific medical treatment was called for but spiritual treatment was the only therapy offered.

Such criticism is neither insubstantial nor over-critical, and one can't help hear echoes of such spiritualizing in Mother Teresa's own words: "Take whatever He gives and give whatever He takes with a big smile" (225).

"Accept everything with a smile" feels like another t-shirt, but the phrase has a distinctly questionable aftertaste because it suggests a willingness to tolerate most any injustice.

She didn't. Mother Teresa famously used her Nobel Prize acceptance speech to warn the world of the evil of abortion. Her crusades on the streets of slums around the world were determined to ease real human suffering. She was the quintessential activist, giving herself away to the cause, *to* Jesus, in the lives of the poor, and *for* Jesus, as a tribute to his great gift.

The late Christopher Hitchens, an atheist and prolific writer, went on the attack against Mother Teresa in a book titled *The Missionary Position: Mother Teresa in theory and practice*. Hitchens' invective is deftly aimed because no Christian believer in the late 20th century was more universally admired. Hitchens' target, he says, is not Mother Teresa per se, but the faith that gave her cause and mission, a faith he famously scorned and ridiculed throughout his life.

"Mother Teresa has a theory of poverty, which is also a theory of submission and gratitude," he writes in the introduction. What most offends his sensibilities is the manner by which she, in his estimation, spiritualized real problems, tried, in a way, to smile away ills in reaching toward some beyond-the-sunset ideal.

That criticism, however misguided and defiantly aimed, is still worth considering. When she tells a dying man, as Hitchens says, "You are suffering like Christ on the cross. So Jesus must be kissing you," it seems to me that Hitchens is not all wrong to call what she's creating a "cult of suffering."

But it's a tough call. How many times aren't we stretched painfully between faithfully relying on God's promises on the one hand and taking extraordinary steps to extend lives on the other? Right at this moment, untold believers in medical offices around the world don't know whether more horrifying chemo or none at all is what God wants.

Too much faith obscures our vision, blinds us to realities. But believing only the realities makes us incapable of seeing anything beyond what is quite literally right there before our eyes.

The eyes of faith require vigilance for this world and the world to come, which is to say, humbly and prayerfully, "*we* do."

Christopher Hitchens wasn't totally wrong about MT and her strategies in helping the oppressed. But all of us – believers and atheists – are beset by dilemmas whose answers and outcomes are vastly more complex and more difficult than any of us – believers and atheists – can quickly and glibly put behind us.

PRAYER: Lord, make us instruments of your will. Help us, guide us, show us the way, especially when the way is dark and difficult, when choices we make are life-and-death. Bless the doctors and nurses – those who serve us and you – as we walk those roads together. Give us clear minds and hearts and feed our souls with your assurance that our answers are yours. Amen.

LXVI. "A CHEERFUL DOG"

A cheerful heart is good medicine, but a crushed spirit dries up the bones. Proverbs 17:22

Cheerfulness is a sign of a generous and mortified person who forgetting all things, even herself, tries to please her God in all she does for souls. Cheerfulness is often a cloak which hides a life of sacrifice, continual union with God, fervor and generosity. A person who has this gift of cheerfulness very often reaches a great height of perfection. For God loves a cheerful giver and He takes close to His heart the religious He loves. (33)

Someone once asked Nelson Mandela, whose years in prison reached despairingly close to a lifetime, why, when finally he was released, he wasn't more angry. Reportedly, he smiled. "If I thought it would be useful," he said, "I would be." A generous spirit was more blessed and more useful.

Cheerfulness had to have been a way of life for Mother Teresa. It had to, for even that immense recognition given to her and her work late in her life was difficult for her accept. She claimed to dislike crowds, and it's clear that she did. She felt uncomfortable with the adulation showered upon her and loved nothing more than returning home after meeting with presidents and potentates and even the pope.

Still, what she found back home in Calcutta was ever more of the dying. She ministered to the lowliest of the low, the most despised – the poor, the infirm, those approaching death totally alone. Her terrain was the torn edge of our existence, the seam where life slips painfully into darkness. The landscape she loved was the beaten shroud of human suffering. The faces she looked into were beautiful only because she saw in them the very image of her suffering Savior.

What's more, impossible as it may seem, she often felt herself despised by God, forgotten, left behind, alone and terrified that the Jesus she so loved had no time for her, her pains or her triumphs. She was, as some call her, a "saint of darkness" (336).

And yet, throughout her life, there is this persistent cheerfulness, this effervescent sense of humor that could, at any moment whatsoever start an entire audience to slapping their knees, or double-up her friends and acquaintances in laughter.

Some of all of that emerged from her belief in providence, in God's own unmistakably cagey guidance. And while some might bicker about God's blessings in this particular situation, Mother Teresa loved the often astonishing juxtaposition of human need and divine largesse. "Three days ago," she once wrote her Archbishop, "we picked up two people eaten alive with worms. The agony of the Cross was on their faces." She says they proceeded to make the two of them comfortable, when one of them, the old man, asked for a cigarette. "How beautiful of God," she says, because "in my bag there were two packets of [the] best cigarettes. . . . God thought of this old man's longing" (254). When with those she served, she seemed never unwilling or unable to smile.

It would be difficult, if not impossible, to nominate a single human being more worthy of the Nobel Peace Prize than Mother Teresa, an award she was given in 1979. In her much heralded – and much hated – acceptance speech in Oslo, Mother Teresa told a story she'd often related elsewhere. She was asked, she said, by a "very big group of professors," to "tell us something that will help us." She told them, in response, simply, to "smile at each other." One of her learned audience must have been a little skeptical. "Are you married?" he asked. "Yes," she told him, without missing a beat, "and I sometimes find it very difficult to smile at Jesus because He can be very demanding" (281).

Or this. She confessed to one of her spiritual directors that she simply lacked the wherewithal to accomplish much: "I can do only one thing, like a little dog following closely the Master's footsteps." And then, "Pray that I be a cheerful dog" (236).

Comparing my suffering to yours or yours to hers is futile. All suffering is suffering. Besides, what good are such comparisons anyway? "It is a curious fact," said Oscar Wilde, "that people are never so trivial as when they take themselves seriously."

Not so, apparently, the cheerful dog.

PRAYER: This morning, Lord, the yard was alive in song – a dozen of your creatures greeting the sun on what feels to be a warm day. Keep us singing, Lord, keep us forever cheerful. No one escapes darkness and tragedy; no one goes home scot free. But through it all, keep us cheerful because we know that in you we have love and life itself. Amen.

LXVII. "Holding God
between my fingers . . ."

"This is my body, which is for you; do this in remembrance of me."
1 Corinthians 11:24

It sounds draconian now, but I remember those Sundays, the Sundays when we celebrated communion, when my father stayed behind after worship to meet with the church consistory and run through the list of members. I was a kid, so I never attended those sessions, but I knew what went on behind closed doors. What the elders tried to determine was who was – and who wasn't – present for the sacrament.

Back then, the church governed far more than what happened on Sunday mornings. The authority of "the church" was formidable, and that may be understatement. It offered untold blessings to those who walked steadfastly on the paths of its righteousness; but, like Dame Fortune of ancient iconography, if she turned her lovely face away, what people saw was yet another face, something altogether hideous.

Some people I know have spent lifetimes licking wounds created by a church determined to identify wheat and chaff, a church that only rarely refused making judgments.

My sense is that era is long gone.

Back then, when the elders did a headcount of who was and who wasn't present for the sacrament, they were making character judgments they believed they had to, given the fact that, on earth, they'd been given special privileges along with what we called "the keys of the kingdom." Furthermore, it was their belief that the supper was, in fact, a "means of grace." Those who weren't present, weren't just skipping church, they were refusing Christ.

Today, those post-worship meetings sound draconian. I honestly doubt that any fellowships practice anything similar today, except perhaps congregations where little or nothing has changed in the last half century, congregations probably slowly dying.

But when I read Mother Teresa on the blessed sacrament, I wonder if my father and his ecclesiastical brothers (not sisters) weren't on to something. After all, what prompted their post-worship headcount was a sacred regard for the sacrament – the bread and wine were not to be missed. Back then, at the evening service, four cordoned-off pews up front, left side, were made available for a repeat if you or your kids were sick in the morning. Communion, a sacrament, was simply not to be missed.

"Some days back – when giving the Holy Communion to our Sisters in the Mother house, suddenly I realized I was holding God between my 2 fingers," Mother Teresa once explained to one of her spiritual guides (283).

There's something about her shocking discovery that is marvelous to me, so rich a realization of the reality of Christ and his gift of the eternity of our existence. In the host, she felt God almighty between her fingers. Amazing.

But it's neither my language nor my experience. And it may never be.

The church I attend these days likes to call the Lord's Supper a feast, a celebration – and it certainly is. We do it more often, too. If people don't come, no one notices. I'm not sure anyone cares. It's all a joy really, a kind of divine party. The wine is gone these days – an AA thing – but the bread is wonderful, homemade, not just Wonder Bread anymore.

At the moment MT determines that God is there between her fingers, she glories in "the greatness of [the] humility of God," she says. "Really no greater love – than the love of Christ" (283).

After all, there he was between her two fingers.

There Jesus was, right there in her hand. That's how immensely low he stoops to conquer.

PRAYER: Your body, broken for us – your blood shed. It's precious beyond our own wildest imagination. Your gift of life is well-supplied with joy and confidence and grace itself. Help us feel it in our hands, in our mouths, in our lives. Make it our treasure because it is, even if we find it so much easier to treasure other things. Love us. Forgive us. Feed us with your body and your spirit. Amen.

LXVIII. "What She Talked About When She Talked About Love"

In Raymond Carver's story, "What We Talk About When We Talk About Love," two couples, in what is shaping up to be an all-nighter, soak themselves in far too much drink while discussing, painfully, what they believe love really means. The discussion turns deadly serious and cold sober when one of them, a cardiologist, talks about an old couple whose broken bodies (they'd been in an accident) required full-body casts. The old man grew depressed, the doctor says, not because of his injuries or hers, but because that body cast's eyeholes simply would not allow him the simple joy of seeing the women he'd loved for so many years.

For a while at least, that love story shuts down their grueling conversation, but my guess is that most retirement home caregivers might just yawn through it because they experience similar stories firsthand most every week, elderly husbands or wives who drive in to convalescent homes and faithfully attend their spouse's every meal despite the fact that their spouse couldn't pick him or her out from a police line.

Dedication. Undying love. Incredible selflessness.

One of the amazing ironies of our culture is that we reward those who take care of our most needy so pitifully.

I don't know why exactly, but lately – when I'm out on the acreage trimming trees or mowing the lawn or doing almost anything – old gospel songs haunt me to the point where I find myself singing through them on some kind of unending loop. Like this one, almost unknown today, but a part of a repertoire I'll never be able to forget:

> Give of your best to the Master;
> Give of the strength of your youth;
> Clad in salvation's full armor,
> Join in the battle for truth.

The conceit that runs through that old hymn was apropos for kids like me, children of war vets: the Christian life as a battle. We're not so keen on the idea any more, which is probably the reason that old hymn has largely disappeared from all but the sealed vault of my memory.

The Sunday school lesson it teaches is a good one – since no one can serve two masters, the scripture says, give of your best to the master, give of "the strength of your youth."

Dedication. Undying love. Incredible selflessness.

I can't say it quite as graphically as Mother Teresa did, but she practiced a devoted sacramentalist faith that's unlike mine, for better or for worse, faith constructed on what she tasted in the blessed sacrament, a rite that infuses the language she offered those who served in her army of care-givers, language like this: "Let the poor and the people eat you up," she told the Sisters in 1984, a vastly more dramatic version of the old hymn's commanding admonition.

> Let the people "bite" your smile, your time. You sometimes might prefer not to even look at somebody when you had some misunderstanding. Then, not only you look, but give a smile. . . . Learn by heart you must let the people eat you up. (285)

I don't think it's possible, really, to offer a way of life that is more patently un-American. We pass along God's own peace most bountifully when we give ourselves away, when we dedicate our undying love in selflessness that's so profound as to die to we are, or want or wish to be, in the name of the Lord Jesus.

"Let the poor and the people eat you up," she said. What she meant was, to them, be the body and the blood. To them, be Jesus.

PRAYER: Strengthen us to weaken us, Lord. Break down our defenses to allow to be shaped only by your will for us. Help us give ourselves away, as you did, in loving us. Teach us to love. Amen.

LXIX. An Open Calvary

"'He will wipe away every tear from their eyes. There will be no more death' or mourning or crying or pain, for the old order of things has passed away." Revelation 21:4

This week there were parents in Moore, Oklahoma, who didn't sleep because their children, their darling school-age children, were trapped somewhere in what little was left of the school where on Tuesday morning, when the bell rang, they'd been sitting in their desks, innocent as doves.

What those moms and dads were going through that night is beyond imagination. They couldn't dig through the rubble themselves because only search-and-rescue people could. All the while, those parents knew the death toll was rising, and no one, right then, had a clear idea where that tally would stop. They could do nothing, absolutely nothing, but cry and pray in a home that must have seemed horrifically empty, as it turned out to be.

And God didn't appear to be helping either. Rain was forecast that next morning, lightning and thunder, even hail. Nothing destructive. On what was left of the streets of Moore, Oklahoma, there was nothing but ruin. Rain wasn't what the searchers needed, nor was it what their kids needed if, by some miracle, they were still alive beneath walls that were no longer walls.

We've got kids in Oklahoma. They're no longer kids, really, but, for a parent, I suppose, they will forever be *kids* – mine. They made it through a horrendous weather week in the Sooner state.

Friends called us, concerned. We could tell them, joyfully, that our kids were untouched, if anyone in the region can be "untouched" by what happened. People knew the elements were conspiring to create a killer cocktail. If you live in Oklahoma, you live with tornadoes.

On my way to my grandchildren's school program that night, I got a call from my mother's pastor, who told me that my mother could use a call from her son because she was deeply concerned – quite emotional – about her grandchildren in Oklahoma. She'd been watching TV.

I hadn't even thought of Mom. So I called her. She's 94. She was worried sick, she said – a heavy dose of all that grief and sadness crept like a storm into her apartment. How could she help not thinking of her grandchildren?

Regardless of when you're reading this, what's beyond doubt is that more disasters, more death, has occurred since a mile-wide tornado ripped an Oklahoma City suburb into shreds in late May, 2013. To all but residents of Moore, what happened this week may well have been forgotten in the storm of tragedies that seem to be our lot as human beings, some of them self-inflicted, others acts of God.

Most everyone I know has a 9/11 story. Those two digits and the slash between them trigger images nearly universal in this country, if not elsewhere. Auschwitz is a word, but it's also much more, a series of black-and-white photographs scarred into the heart and mind. Whole sections of hurricane-ravaged New Orleans have yet to be rebuilt.

On Christmas, 1984, Mother Teresa stood on the streets of Addis Ababa, Ethiopia, totally overwhelmed by the poverty – "I have never seen so much suffering," she wrote to Father van der Peet. This woman, who had lived her life among the poorest of the poor, claimed what she'd seen that day, the day of the birth of Jesus, was what she called "an open Calvary," a place where "the Passion of Christ was being relived in the bodies of crowds & crowds of people" (308).

Briarwood Elementary School, Moore, Oklahoma, 2013

An open Calvary.

I don't doubt for a moment that's what she would have seen in the faces of those parents of lost children in Moore, Oklahoma, this week, another "open Calvary," in the anxiety and then grief of moms and dads whose sweet kids never left Plaza Towers Elementary School, kids who that first night would have still been there – if they weren't already with the Lord.

Some say it was the biggest tornado ever. A couple dozen people died in that storm, several of them children.

I'd like to say those kids belong to all of us, but they don't. Mine are safe.

Theirs are part of an open Calvary all of us have seen at one time or another in our lives, but most of us will never forget.

God, have mercy. Lord, have mercy.

PRAYER: Lord, right at this moment bless those who are besieged with the kind of grief that overwhelms, the grief that rises unbidden and unforeseen in the lives of all of us, that leaves us speechless, breathless, in its awful wake. There are many, Lord, right at this moment, who find themselves hopeless in an open Calvary. Bless them with your presence. Amen.

LXX. Peace

For to us a child is born, to us a son is given, and the government will be on his shoulders. And he will be called Wonderful Counselor, Mighty God, Everlasting Father, Prince of Peace. Isaiah 9:6

God allowed me to begin my repentance in this way: when I lived in sin, seeing lepers was a very bitter experience for me. God himself guided me into their midst and among them I performed acts of charity. What appeared bitter to me became sweetness of the soul and body.

If you believe this line is unquestionably Mother Teresa's, you're mistaken. But it's not difficult to understand how she might have said it. It's actually St. Francis of Assisi's own story, the story of his conversion. It could well have been MT's. She might well have used his words.

Right now, at this very moment, there's a scrubby cottontail nibbling at half-a-pan full of kernel corn just outside the patio door. His ears are perked, and he's munching like an idiot, filling his belly. I have no idea if it's a he, but the silly thing is cute as the dickens. He's looking right at me, ten feet away.

There's a fence up around our tomatoes to keep him and his cohorts out. If that fence wouldn't be there and wouldn't be a couple feet tall, our tomatoes would be munched to nubbins. I know a ton of friends who keep a .22 just inside the door, just for bunnies.

On the bird feeder outside, there's an indigo bunting right now, a bird whose radiant blue plumage seems cartoon-like, something one could buy in a Hallmark store and then stick, for show, in a bouquet of lilacs. Just a few moments ago, an oriole sat on a ledge picking at an orange I put up there.

St. Francis – Mother Teresa's inspiration – had a thing for animals. He claimed to talk to them. One of the most memorable stories of his life concerns the manner by which he lectured a wolf who was terrorizing the village – *lectured*, as in "explained diligently." The story goes that he told the wolf to stop praying on the townspeople, his finger right there in the wolf's face. Then, reportedly, he told the town that that beast's appetite would dissipate if they fed it – so they did. Years later, when the animal died, the village mourned.

We're talking 13ᵗʰ century AD, here, so that whole story is not on YouTube. What's beyond question, however, is how much St. Francis of Assisi would love the animal circus going on right now outside my window this early June morning.

Contemporarily, St. Francis is likely most heralded for becoming the namesake of the new Pope. I don't doubt that Amazon has seen his biographies surge or spike in the last few months. Before that, what most all believers knew about him was his prayer for peace, the prayer Mother Teresa herself used at the outset of the speech she gave when accepting the Nobel Peace Prize: "Lord, make me an instrument of your peace. . . ." Most of us, Protestant and Catholic, know much of that famous prayer. Legions of believers have it up on their walls in brilliant cross-stitch. Thousands of variations come up when it's Googled.

Mother Teresa's take on peace became one of her most famous creations, offered to the Missionaries of Charity on January 31, 1980.

The fruit of silence is prayer,
The fruit of prayer is faith,
The fruit of faith is love,
The fruit of love is service,
The fruit of service is peace. (315)

To read the story of Mother Teresa is to stretch one's understanding of what some call the radical character of the Christian life. What she valued is a package of behavior that cost both nothing and everything. You can't buy love or faith; you can only give it away. In economic terms, it's perfectly worthless; but, if you believe her – and St. Francis – life without those qualities is poverty, even madness.

MT's patron saint hung out with wolves and spoke to indigo buntings – and probably bunnies too. He believed Christ was there in the minds and hearts and faces of lepers, of those without hope. He believed in peace.

So did she, the kind of peace that passes all understanding.

I wonder if she knew the words of the hymn we sang yesterday in church: "– in peace that only Thou canst give, / With thee, O Master, let me live."

Whether she could hum the tune is questionable, but I have no doubt she knew the words.

PRAYER: Lord, make me an instrument of your peace,
Where there is hatred, let me sow love;
Where there is injury, pardon;
Where there is doubt, faith;
Where there is despair, hope;
Where there is darkness, light;
Where there is sadness, joy. Amen.

LXXI. Champion

Not long ago, a man named Paul Tudor Jones, a gadzillionaire hedge fund manager in a forum of other mega-rich men round-tabling on the campus of a major university, took a question from the audience, from a woman who wondered why all the panelists were silver-haired gents – and there were no such women. Pity poor, rich Mr. Jones. He tried to give the best answer he knew, but he could not for the life of him reverse the direction of that foot of his he'd placed so eagerly in his mouth.

Because women have babies, he said; and once women hold those darling newborns to their "bosoms" [his word], they lose their sharpness, a sharpness prerequisite to hedge fund management. Women are, by nature, wired to love the little ones they bring into the world. They're lost to the trade because those babies disorient the laser-like commitments required to make really, really big money.

He may be right. I've always believed female perception differs from male perception, always felt gender differences to be as mysterious as they are real. But there's something terribly offensive about what Mr. Jones said and how he said it, something that snorts like a pig of the male chauvinist breed.

He's stereotyping women, of course, and slighting both sexes – isn't a man different too once he becomes a father? What's more, the sexism inherent in the answer he gave suggests exactly why there aren't more women hedge-fund fat cats? – the attitudes like Mr. Jones all too brashly trumpeted.

But there's more. In the broadest sense, the equation he created with his answer goes like this: one can choose to love money *or* children. If you want to be me up here around this fancy table, he might have said, you got to love money, with all your heart, with all your soul, and with all your mind. And, oh yeah, to heck with the neighbors.

I once knew a man so committed to being a novelist that he told others, including his wife, that nothing – absolutely nothing – would stand in his way. He wrote novels all right – more than twenty; but when he died, he died alone. If you want to read those novels, you can still get some of them used, from Amazon. They're out of print.

Was he a better novelist for committing the way he did to his craft?

Can someone be a great mathematician if her motivation isn't fever-pitched? When eight-year-old gymnasts show the kind of natural talent only Olympians have, they're quickly escorted into worlds different from anything their third-grade classmates will ever know. Is there any other way to be a champion than to give everything?

He may be right.

At eighty years old, burdened with health problems, subject to taxing exhaustion of constant travel, surrounded always by admirers and yet somehow bereft of the love of Christ Jesus, Mother Teresa still rose daily at 4:40 in the morning just to be among the very first into the chapel for morning prayers. Her commitment was total, even when her spirit faltered.

No one could have given more. No one so entirely gave herself away. No one's commitment was so iron-clad.

But then, she was convinced that she saw in the minds and eyes and hearts of the poor nothing less than her Lord and Savior Jesus Christ. He may not have been in her heart – at least that's what she believed; but he was always there in the visage of the powerless, the dying, the emaciated face of the poor.

With her selfless commitment she might have made one of America's finest hedge fund managers; but thank the Lord that with indefatigable commitment to smile, to love, to feed, and to clothe, she choose something vastly different than making money.

She was, without a doubt, a champion of faith.

LXXII. Home

This is how we know what love is: Jesus laid down his life for us. And we ought to lay down our lives for our brothers and sisters. 1 John 3:16

The Reverend Stephen R. Riggs died in 1883, many years before I was born. I didn't know him – I couldn't have. He may have had an acidic personality – I don't know. He may have mistreated his wife with, at best, inattention. He was a preacher, but he may well have been ornery as a junkyard dog.

But from what I know about him, I respect him. He played an unimaginably significant role in an American horror story, the Dakota War of 1862, a bloody legacy that still haunts the state of Minnesota, where it happened. Hundreds died, and 38 Dakota men were hanged in the largest mass execution in American history.

Riggs was no saint, at least no one has ever canonized him. He did almost unforgiveable things during the Dakota War, like, without doing any significant investigation, bringing almost instantaneous charges against Dakota men accused of rape and murder, charges that resulted in death by hanging.

I still respect him. He may well have been wrong, but his story is a human story of perseverance. He started a ministry among the Dakota in the Minnesota River valley in the 1830s; by the time of the Dakota War, he and his wife had been there for decades. He translated portions of the Bible into the Dakota language, a language that hadn't been written before he started work. You can still buy his Dakota grammar on Amazon.

After the war, when Minnesota's white folks wanted all of the Native people – even the Ojibwe, who hadn't been involved – dead or deported, Riggs was a tireless advocate. When Native suffering became unbearable – hundreds died – he was there beside them, helping.

But most of all I respect him for staying, for making his mission into something more than a mission. Really, Stephen R. Riggs never left the field. He may have come to Dakota country on a mission, but it wasn't a mission – it was his life. He stayed with the Sioux; he moved to South Dakota, but he didn't leave, and neither did his children. He didn't retire to Ohio, from whence he came. He stayed.

There are, of course, different definitions of *mission*. In war, a *mission* might well be to secure a perimeter or capture a bridge, to free hostages or destroy an airfield, in other words, an important but temporary action: *mission*, a specific action to be accomplished.

But *mission* refers to something larger too, a statement of purpose or, even more broadly, a reason for existence.

By the end of her life, Mother Teresa was, by all measures, a celebrity. What she said made news, where she traveled there were crowds. The Missionaries of Charity were still her people, but she'd become a star.

But what I'll always respect about her is what everyone around her knew: no matter where she traveled or who she met or how many networks carried her picture, she loved nothing better than coming home.

When, as a girl, she went to India, she went to war all right – war against poverty and loneliness and fear. Her mission was to destroy the darkness that people experience when all they see before them is a curtain – life or death without love.

But *mission* wasn't something she intended to accomplish, only to return to the home place in Skopje, Albania, or some adorable little flat in Rome with a nice view of the Vatican. Calcutta was home, the streets of the city she'd walked for so many years. Once Mother Teresa started her mission, she never left the home place.

Missionaries come in all sizes, of course, and perfectly understandable reasons exist for leaving the field when it's impossible to stay. And there are innumerable reasons to canonize Mother Teresa – her life was a gift not just to the poor she served in Calcutta, but to all of us.

But I think the crowning glory of what she did is that she never once saw her mission as something to be accomplished. She lived where she served. She never left. The people she served were her neighbors, her brothers and sisters. Her mission was her home.

Praise be to God.

PRAYER: Lord, thank you for Mother Teresa – her life, her story, her commitment, her saintliness. Thank you for giving the world such an incredible emblem of commitment to faith and truth, to you. Bless us with the gift she's given us, the gift of deep abiding faith that our work is yours. Amen.

Illustrations by Chapter

1. Mother Teresa, photo © 1986 by Túrelio (https://commons.wikimedia. org/wiki/File:MotherTeresa_090.jpg [CC-BY-SA-2.0 de])

4. Sitting Bull (1831–1890), PD (Public Domain)

9. JCS

12. Anne Frank school photo (1940), PD

14. JCS

16. Rev. Leonard Verduin, JCS

17. Crucifix, JCS

23. Mississippi John Hurt, PD

27. JCS

28. Zuni Mission, Zuni Pueblo, NM, circa 1935, JCS

30. Joseph Smith, PD

33. The hungry of Calcutta, PD

34. A Lakota giveaway, PD

38. Mother Teresa, photo by Manfredo Ferrari (https://commons.wikimedia. org/wiki/File:Mutter_Teresa_von_Kalkutta.jpg [CC BY-SA 4.0)

43. Pieter Bruegel the Elder: The Seven Deadly Sins or the Seven Vices – Pride. PD

44. Andrew and Effa Vander Wagen, JCS

50. Abraham Kuyper, PD

51. Mother Teresa, Khayalitsha, Cape Town, JCS

53. From Robert Vignola's 1934 film *The Scarlet Letter*, CC photo by JCavett22 (https://www.flickr.com/photos/43344526@N08/3985223169/ [CC BY 2.0])

55. Martin Luther, PD

57. Photo of Pope Benedict XVI by Fabio Pozzebom for Agência Brasil (https://commons.wikimedia.org/wiki/File:BentoXVI-51-11052007.jpg [CC BY 3.0 BR] – cropped)

59. Adirondack chairs, Bread Loaf, Vermont, JCS

62. Mother Teresa, photo © 1986 by Túrelio (https://commons.wikimedia.org/wiki/File:MotherTeresa_094.jpg [CC-BY-SA-2.0 de]

64. JCS

69. 2013 Moore tornado damage at Briarwood Elementary School, EF5 rated by NWS WFO Norman, OK, PD.

71. Memorial plaque dedicated to Mother Teresa by Otilie Šuterová-Demelová at building in Václavské náměstí square in Olomouc (Czech Republic), photo by Michal Maňas (https://commons.wikimedia.org/wiki/File:Mother_Teresa_memorial_plaque.jpg [CC BY 2.5])

CPSIA information can be obtained at www.ICGtesting.com
Printed in the USA
LVOW11s0146291115

464137LV00001B/1/P